HotPots

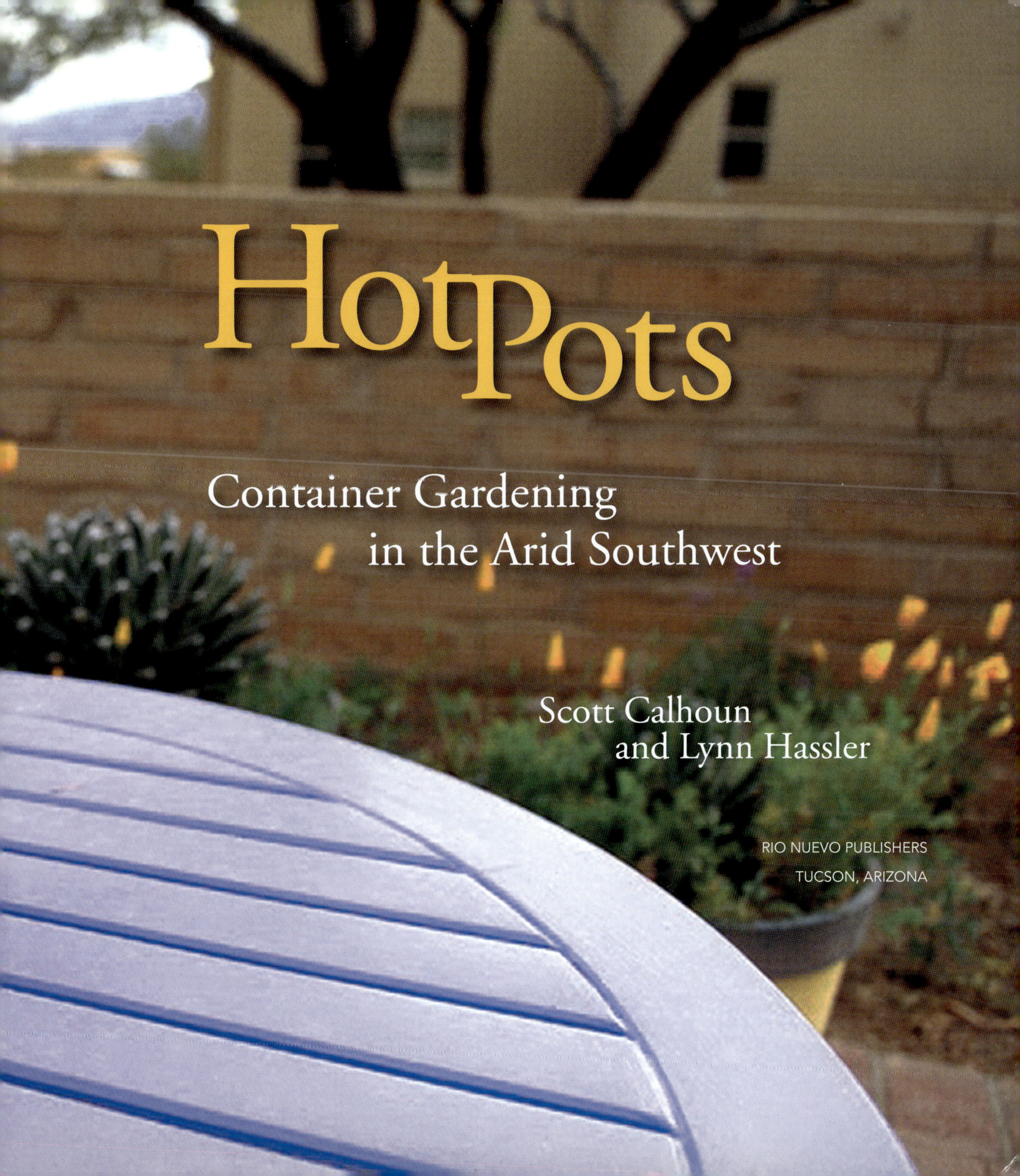

Hot Pots

Container Gardening in the Arid Southwest

Scott Calhoun
and Lynn Hassler

RIO NUEVO PUBLISHERS
TUCSON, ARIZONA

INTRODUCTION 7

CHAPTER 1. SELECTING POTS 15

Containers that "Breathe"? 15

Types of Container Materials 16

Hanging Containers for Hot, Dry Climates: Rat-tails, Donkey's Tails, and Elephant's Food 19

What About Strawberry Jars? 20

Talavera Pottery 21

Recycled Materials 22

Pots on the Move: Relocating Your Containers 24

Criteria for Pot Selection 26

Pots on High 29

Collection Saucers 30

Pot Temperature 30

CHAPTER 2. DESIGNING WITH POTS 35

Monopotting and Staging Specimen Plants 36

Contemporary Staging 38

Pot Placement Ideas 39

Pottery Artist: Mike Cone 42

Pottery Artist: Jan Bell 43

CHAPTER 3. PLANTS 45

Sculptural Plants 45

Sculptural Plant Charts 56

Succulent Bulbs 62

Perennials for Potted Pizzazz 64

Annual Color: A New Look for Every Season 72

Urban Herbs 80

A Moveable Feast: Veggies in Containers 86

CHAPTER 4. SOILS 93

The Dirt on Dirt 93

Common Potting Mix Ingredients 95

Concocting Your Own Mix 96

Soil Mixes from the Experts 97

The Life of a Soil Mix 97

CHAPTER 5. CARE AND FEEDING 101

Watering Frequency 102

A Few Watering Tips 105

Using Drip 106

Fertilizing 107

Root Bound! 108

Up Potting 108

CHAPTER 6. FINISHING TOUCHES 111

Top Dressing and Mulch for Pots 111

Accessorizing to Perk Up Your Pots 115

Labeling Your Plants 115

HOT POT

RESOURCES 119

GENERAL INDEX 122

INDEX OF PLANT

NAMES 122

THYME
OREGANO
orégano
Cilantro

ABOVE: Cool silver Parry's agave (*Agave parryi*) in a bright green pot.

LEFT: Herbs grown in recycled cinder blocks.

INTRODUCTION

When it comes to gardening in containers in the Southwest, you can forget most of what you've read in books from other regions. For this arid land, books from England on container gardening are about as useful as muck boots in Phoenix. In the Southwest, sculptural plants are the true superstars of pot culture. Because of an unmatched selection of succulent plants suited to containers, gardeners who delight in using plants as living sculptures will be spoiled by choice here. As for annuals, perennials, herbs, and vegetables, you will find some familiar selections, but often with different planting times. Given relatively mild temperatures throughout the year, it's relatively easy to plan for year-round bloom here. An added bonus to container gardening in the Southwest is that gardeners can leave their prized pots outdoors year-round; in colder regions, pots must be hauled indoors each winter to protect them from frigid conditions.

WHY GARDEN IN CONTAINERS?

Besides being lots of fun, container gardening affords us flexibility, control, opportunities for creativity, and relative ease in terms of daily chores. It also allows us to maximize our individual microclimates (small hot or cool zones around the house).

Flexibility and Mobility without Yoga Classes

Gardening in containers is something that can be done almost anywhere—on a balcony, small patio, or along a front entryway. Since yard space seems to be shrinking in new housing developments across the Southwest, space-saving containers are often the perfect solution. Container gardening enables us to enjoy plants in areas where traditional gardens might not be possible. It also allows us more flexibility in terms of plant placement. Potted plants are relatively easy to move and can be shifted around for whatever reasons—climate concerns, aesthetics, or sheer boredom—not to mention the fact that they can be moved along with you if you relocate. If a plant is dormant in winter, for example, and you don't wish to add annuals or some other material to liven up the container, simply move the unsightly pot out of view. Of course, an empty pot is not necessarily unsightly. Some empty pots are so attractive that they can be placed into a garden as a sculpture sans plants.

Control Issues

We all like to feel like we are in charge, and gardening in containers affords us more control over growing conditions. Pot gardening allows us to select specific soil mixes, determine moisture levels, and manage temperature conditions much better than if we were planting in the ground. If a plant fails to thrive in one location, we can simply move it to another—a slightly different light orientation might make all the difference in the world.

A Vessel for Your Creativity

When you garden with pots, the container becomes a bonus design element. By experimenting with different combinations of plants and pots, it's possible to create highly individualized—and sometimes unexpected—combinations of texture, sculptural form, color, and drama. Some pots are design elements in themselves and can stand alone without any plants at all. Containers can be elegant, quirky, or just downright functional. Cluster different types together to achieve varying effects. By using pots of different heights, you can change the visual topography of an otherwise flat garden.

Ease

Watering issues aside, container gardening may actually be easier than in-ground gardening. Certainly less digging is required, as well as less stooping for weeding, watering, and fertilizing. Placing pots on tables, plant stands, or against walls makes them easier for us to reach—and they are less likely to be raided by local wildlife such as rabbits or javelinas. Containers that are tall in stature may also protect plants from marauding critters. Watering can be relatively effortless when pots are grouped closely together.

Maximizing Microclimates

Every garden has certain locations within the larger surrounding area that have slightly different climates. These are called microclimates. Some spots may be extra chilly; others may be very hot, often due to the proximity of buildings, driveways, patios, or other hardscape. Some sites receive more wind protection than others if located near a dense row of shrubs or an adobe wall. The ability to move plants into different microclimates in any season is a real plus in this land of temperature extremes. Remember that high spots are warmer than low spots and that pots placed along south- and west-facing walls

Red yucca and bidens mingle in this recyled mining bin which serves as a focal point in the courtyard. Design: Greg Corman.

or buildings will absorb heat from them and stay warmer. Pots placed along northern exposures will receive a lot of shade for most of the year but can get late afternoon sun in the summer.

CHALLENGES, REALITIES, AND MINOR DOWNSIDES

Moisture (or Lack Thereof)

In the arid Southwest, we can't simply leave our container plants outside hoping it will rain. Most of the region lacks sufficient natural rainfall to water container or in-ground gardens. Average annual rainfalls are meager—less than 16 inches. Long periods of time pass between rains, making supplemental watering a way of life. In addition, annual evaporation exceeds the annual rainfall, presenting all kinds of trials and tribulations for living things. Add drying winds to the mix, and it's clear that this is a land of gardening challenges. Most of the year is dry with low humidity, but in July, August, and September, the summer monsoon moves into many areas with a vengeance. Humidity increases, and daily showers are often the norm. Watering schedules need to be adjusted in order to prevent root rot from too much moisture.

Cold

In the lower deserts of the Southwest, we can expect two to fourteen nights of freezing weather each winter. Cold temperatures can limit the amount of plant growth even more than heat and is an important consideration when situating containers. For plants that will not tolerate frost, consider placing (or temporarily moving) them under covered porches. Use frost cloth to cover plants that can't be moved; it provides an extra 2–4 degrees F of protection on cold nights.

LEFT: Bougainvillea can be flamboyant against a sunny wall.

BELOW: Water 'Blue Elf' aloe (*Aloe* x 'Blue Elf') lightly during the heat of summer.

Heat

Even though freezing temperatures may be our first concern, extreme heat affects plants as well. When summer temperatures rise above 105 degrees F, the roots of many succulents simply shut down, and if overwatered during this time, plant roots may rot. During these particularly hot times, it's best to water succulents with the same frequency as you normally would, but to water *lightly.* Although this method may sound counterintuitive to the conventional wisdom that says that pots should be watered thoroughly until water comes out the drainage holes, for winter-growing succulents—particularly aloes—this light watering technique is an effective strategy. Light watering provides plants with enough moisture to survive, but not the excessive amount that can rot roots. For other types of plants, the conventional wisdom works just fine.

Light

The Southwest is a land filled with light, and the overabundance of it presents some challenges when selecting plants and deciding where to place them. When considering where to situate a particular plant, look at its leaf color for a clue. Plants with gray-green, silver, or blue-gray leaves are generally very tolerant of sun; leaves with these colors help to reflect sunlight. Cactus species with dense spines, especially white spines, are fully adapted to bright sunlight; the spines actually provide shade for the plant. On the other hand, plants with dark green leaves usually prefer some shade, especially during midday

Even in the desert, winter temperatures get cold enough to damage some frost-sensitive plants.

and afternoon. Many leafy plants (most perennials, annuals, and some herbs and veggies) prefer an eastern exposure with morning sun and afternoon shade since glaring sunlight can literally burn leaves and stems.

Minor Downsides

As with all things in life, there are some downsides to gardening in containers. Because a pot has limited soil space, root systems are restricted; they can outgrow a container in no time flat. When you see roots coming out the drainage hole and/or notice that your plants are failing to thrive, it may mean that the plant has literally outgrown its pot. At this point, the plant will need to be transferred to a larger container. Limited space also increases a container's heat load. Sometimes plants grown in containers are more short-lived than in-ground plants. Plants in pots often require more constant care—which actually might be considered a positive thing if you really enjoy bonding with your plants. Since containers dry out rapidly, vigilant watering is necessary; during the summer months, a skipped day of watering can mean death for certain plants. Frequent watering can also lead to higher mineral and salt buildup in the soil. Because continual watering washes out nutrients, fertilizing becomes important and must be done on a more regular basis. Seeping water and fertilizer can stain patios or other surfaces. Highly glazed, dark-colored pots can cook plant roots. But please realize that many of these disadvantages can be dealt with quite easily by choosing appropriate containers and appropriate plant materials.

So let's end this section on a positive note. Containers filled with plants can soften a hardscape or brighten an area that seems dull in any season. You may start out simply, purchasing one attractive container and filling it with a single plant that serves as a focal point for your patio or courtyard. But over time you may find yourself getting more ambitious: acquiring more and more pots, selecting from a wide array of materials and colors that suit your tastes, trying different plant combinations, and playing with form, texture, and color. Container gardening can become rather addicting—more so now than ever before because of the vast array of choices in terms of pot and plant selection. Some people have been known to fill their entire backyards with container plantings.

LEFT: La Paloma, an import shop in Tubac, Arizona, offers a wide selection of colorful containers.

CHAPTER 1:

Selecting Pots

HISTORICALLY, GARDENING AFICIONADOS used whatever objects were on hand for "containing" their plants. At the University of Arizona in Tucson, old coffee cans with holes punched in their bottoms were the first homes for many of the plants now growing on campus. Essentially the item itself really didn't matter as long as it was sturdy enough to hold soil and roots and would not tip over.

It was sometime in the 1940s that plastic pots and potting mixes became widely available, and container gardening has been increasing in popularity ever since. Today, many different kinds of containers, made from an array of materials, are commercially available.

CONTAINERS THAT "BREATHE?"

You may have heard gardeners talking about certain kinds of containers that either "breathe" or "don't breathe." What this refers to is the porosity of a pot. If a container is porous, it means that water and air can easily penetrate and move about, enabling plant roots to get plenty of oxygen. Because porous containers can "breathe," they

ABOVE: Terra-cotta pots come in many shapes and sizes.

BELOW RIGHT: Hypertufa troughs are perfect for highlighting a succulent collection.

What "Ting" and "Thud" Mean: is My Pot High- or Low-fired?

How does one distinguish between low-fired and high-fired terra-cotta containers? Low-fired pots make a dull "thud" when you tap on them with your fingers; high-fired pots produce more of a"ting" sound. Also, look for terra-cotta pots with thicker walls for a longer life span.

don't stay soggy. But this also means that they will dry out rather quickly, a point of concern in our hot, dry climate. Those ever-popular terra-cotta pots, available everywhere, are porous, as are paper pulp pots and untreated wood containers.

Nonporous containers do not allow for the free passage of air and moisture. The soil within the pot tends to retain moisture, so it's important to provide good drainage and avoid overwatering and overfeeding. While moisture retention may be an advantage for some plants in hot climates, nonporous pots are not a good choice for cacti or succulents, or other plants requiring very little water. Some containers that are considered nonporous include plastic, glazed ceramic, fiberglass, concrete, and metal.

TYPES OF CONTAINER MATERIALS

Terra-cotta

Traditionally, clay pots have been the most popular for container planting. Clay pots come unglazed or glazed. The term *terra cotta* comes from Latin and literally means "cooked earth." Terra-cotta containers are made from unglazed clay, then fired in a kiln. They are brick red or buff-colored and are generally machine-made and mass-produced, although some hand-thrown varieties are available as well. Terra-cotta containers are porous, which means the soil will dry out quickly. Depending on the type of plant used in these pots, frequent watering may be required. Salts and minerals from water and fertilizers often wick outward to collect on these containers and may cause white stains. Terra-cotta containers can be fragile and may crack in a freeze.

If you like the look of terra-cotta, be aware of differences in quality. Some terra-cotta pots produced in Mexico, China, or Thailand are fired at low temperatures, and peeling and chipping are the result. Some of these pots may be painted with a black substance inside (a sort of tar called asphalt emulsion), which can help with the problem. However, the paint used is petroleum-based, and thus they are not a suitable choice for growing edible plants. It is also possible to treat terra-cotta with a vinyl sealant, applied both inside and outside the pot, in order to extend its life. Some people apply an asphalt roofing compound on the inside; again, this is not appropriate for plants you plan to eat. Italian terra-cotta pots are more uniform and higher in quality and are not coated with asphalt roofing compound; however, like all terra-cotta pots, they will wick water and are susceptible to frost damage.

Ceramic

Ceramic pots are made from clay that has been glazed. Containers in this category give a more finished appearance than terra-cotta, and often provide a design element in themselves, whether planted or not. They come in a wide range of colors and shapes, providing endless creative possibilities. Unlike unglazed clay, which allows water and air to pass through, glazed clay restricts the movement of water and air. Ceramic containers are nonporous, so they hold moisture longer. This may be an advantage for certain types of plants, but be careful not to overwater or overfertilize. Also note that glazed pots absorb more heat from direct sunlight than unglazed pots. You don't want to "cook" your roots.

Plastic

Plastic containers tend to be less expensive than ceramic but lack a certain substance. They often look, well, "plasticky" or stated more plainly, cheap. While practical because of their light weight, plastic pots are usually not the most attractive-looking selections, but it's always possible to place a planted plastic pot into a larger, more showy-looking container. Plastic does not insulate well and can heat up and burn roots. Because plastic containers are not porous, overwatering can be a problem. They are not a good choice for cacti or succulents. But some plants do benefit from the plastic pot's ability to hold water longer. Pots made of plastic are much less likely to crack than clay pots. Some newer thermoplastic materials—often called "resin planters"—give the look of a terracotta or ceramic pot without the weight and might be the best choice in the plastic category.

TOP: This highly glazed pot is a piece of art in its own right and stands alone without any plant material.

ABOVE: Parry's agave with chunky riprap mulch.

Beaked yucca and Weber's agave work to excellent effect in this elevated metal saucer planting at Big Red Sun Nursery in Austin, Texas.

Metal

Containers made from iron, steel, aluminum, copper, zinc, or lead can add a unique look to your potted garden. Since iron rusts, you might consider painting it to protect it from water, though some people like the rusted look. Stainless steel does not rust. Aluminum usually develops a white surface coating, which appeals to some. Be aware that metal absorbs heat, so keep these containers out of hot sun to avoid root damage. Metal containers are often used as cachepots with other containers inside (see "Pot within a Pot" sidebar on page 21).

Fiberglass

Fiberglass containers are mid-priced, lighter-weight than plastic, strong, and attractive. They are nonporous, so they hold moisture longer. They also insulate well, so roots are cooler in summer and warmer in winter. Fiberglass, often a gray stone color, holds up well to the elements and does not fade, chip, or crack.

Wood

Wood containers are porous unless treated with a waterproofing sealer. While half-whiskey barrels may be tempting, wood is simply not a good choice for our climate. The continual watering necessary for maintaining plant life here breaks this medium down quickly. Increased humidity during the monsoon also contributes to its demise. All wood rots over time in the presence of water and soil microorganisms.

Stone

Stone containers look solid and are expensive and nonporous. Of all the container materials currently available, they are the most durable but also the heaviest. Weight can be a problem in certain settings. A calcareous limestone material called "cantera" stone is often sold in the Southwest and is a good choice for rustic Mexican-style planters.

Cast Concrete

Cast concrete is a less expensive substitute for stone. Molded to form planters, these make heavy, durable containers. They are nonporous. Note that dark-colored concrete will absorb more heat.

Container Types at a Glance

Terra-cotta (unglazed clay): heavy, porous, some low-fired varieties break down easily

Ceramic (glazed clay): more finished appearance, heavy, nonporous, absorbs heat

Plastic: lightweight, nonporous, non-insulating, relatively durable

Metal: weight depends on metal, nonporous, absorbs heat

Fiberglass: lightweight, nonporous, durable

Wood: keeps soil temperatures fairly even, porous even with sealer treatment, short-lived

Stone: heavy, nonporous, expensive

Cast concrete: heavy and durable, nonporous

Hypertufa: lightweight, porous, not readily available commercially

Hypertufa

Hypertufa containers combine the porosity of clay with the attractive look of stone, as well as the value of concrete. Hypertufa is a type of artificial stone that was developed as a substitute for the natural volcanic lightweight rock called tufa, a spongy cellular rock found in areas with limestone. It was first created in the 19th century and used for making alpine-style planting troughs. Made from varying combinations of dry cement, peat moss, sand, perlite or vermiculite, and water, hypertufa containers are loved by rock gardeners and cactus/succulent aficionados; they can be grouped together to mimic rocky landscape settings.

HANGING CONTAINERS FOR HOT, DRY CLIMATES: RAT-TAILS, DONKEY'S TAILS, AND ELEPHANT'S FOOD

Increased air circulation coupled with extremely hot temperatures is a recipe for disaster in "hanging basket"-style containers. The sphagnum moss-lined hanging planters that you see in other parts of the country are simply not practical in our dry climate. They are almost impossible to keep sufficiently watered during the long warm season. Hanging plastic containers may work for some seasonal annuals, but they dry out more quickly than you think, requiring twice daily watering (at the very least!) in the hottest part of the summer.

RIGHT: A tree festooned with burro tail at Lotusland in Santa Barbara.

BELOW: Who needs strawberries? Succulents are a better choice in arid climates. Design: Hacienda del Sol Guest Ranch Resort.

On the other hand, some cacti and succulents lend themselves to hanging containers and don't require much water at all. Try one of the following:

- **Donkey or Burro Tail** (*Sedum morganianum*) Protect from frost and give it morning sun only in warmer months.
- **Elephant's Food** (*Portulacaria afra*) Grow in sun or shade, protect from frost.
- **Rat-tail Cactus** (*Aporocactus flagelliformis*) Beware of frost and protect from full afternoon sun in warm season to enjoy its bright pink flowers.

WHAT ABOUT STRAWBERRY JARS?

Strawberry jars are usually made from terra-cotta but are fired in the kiln at higher temperatures. Glazed varieties are now available as well. Strawberry jars are generally round in shape and have several planting pockets. Originally designed to accommodate trailing strawberry plants, these pots make attractive design elements. Since actual strawberry plants are a poor choice for growing in the desert Southwest, try planting them with succulents instead. Many fleshy-leafed plants are well adapted to these containers. Consider hens and chicks (*Echeveria* spp.), elephant's food (*Portulacaria afra*), or candelilla (*Euphorbia antisyphilitica*). Strawberry pots look attractive when planted with clumping or trailing seasonal annuals, and some herbs also work well. But be sure to pay attention to the watering, for these pots are often relatively small and will dry out quickly. Strawberry pots may look quite empty and sparse when initially planted, but the plants will fill in over time.

How to Plant a Strawberry Jar

Begin by placing screening or loose-fitting rock over the drainage hole. Add potting mix and gently firm it to just below the level of the lowest pocket(s). After gently loosening roots, place plants in these low openings and then arrange soil mix around roots and into center of the jar. Repeat until you have planted all of the pockets; then continue as you would with a regular container, filling soil to within inches of the top. If you attempt to fill the entire pot with soil mix before planting, you'll end up pushing the soil mix out the sides and over the top of the container, and it will be difficult to position the plants in the lower pockets. Water thoroughly both from the top of the container and through the planting pockets.

TALAVERA POTTERY

Talavera pots are some of the most attractive containers on the market today. Talavera is tin-enameled earthenware that is produced in Puebla, Mexico, an area with abundant supplies of clay. It is believed that the particular techniques for making this type of pottery were introduced in Puebla by immigrants from Talavera de la Reina, Spain; hence the name. Although the indigenous people of Mexico were already accomplished potters with a long tradition of producing earthenware, the arrival of the Spaniards introduced

Pot within a Pot

You can always place a less attractive pot inside a slightly larger, more elegant-looking one. This is called cachepotting. Cachepots are decorative pots or jars used for holding potted plants. "Cache" is from the French word *cacher,* meaning "to hide."

ABOVE: Big pink pincushion (*Mammillaria guelzowiana*) brings a pop of hot pink to this Talavera pot.

BELOW: Bishop's cap cactus in a rusted gas can.

BELOW RIGHT: A washtub with medicinal aloe and glass and tile makes an excellent focal point.

them to two new concepts: the potter's wheel and tin-based glaze. In the beginning, all Talavera pots were made in tones of white and blue. However, in the 18th century new colors were introduced, and today Talavera comes in a vast array of color combinations.

The basic process for making Talavera pottery remains essentially the same as it was in the 16th century, though there have been many changes in terms of shape and style. It's made with two types of clay, a dark variety and a lighter, slightly rose-colored clay; both come from the state of Puebla. The two are mixed together, strained, and kneaded. Each item is modeled by hand, turned on the wheel or pressed in a mold, then left to dry for 50–90 days. Once dry, pots are fired and then hand-dipped in a glaze which forms the white background of the design. Stencil designs are then dusted into place with charcoal powder. Each piece is hand painted and fired for a second time at a higher temperature.

RECYCLED MATERIALS

In traditional Mexican-American households, when an object lost its usefulness in the house, it often found new life in the garden as a container for plants. While more formal gardeners might be reluctant to use recycled materials for planting, many gardeners recognize the creative potential offered by using "old junk" as a planting medium. There is

ABOVE: A golden barrel in a chair makes for a witty garden ornament. Design: Dan Johnson.

LEFT: Recycle an old chair to display your potted plants.

Pot Fountains

Curvaceous urn-shaped pots have become a hot item for gardeners seeking small elegant fountains. The basic idea is this: you take the urn and plumb it with pipe through its drain hole and suspend it over a sealed basin via a grate. The basin is below grade and the basin and grate are covered with rocks at grade. A recalculating pump pushes the water up into the urn and when it is full the water flows over the rim, down the sides, through the grate and back into the basin where it is recirculated.

no shortage of possible containers: old buckets, large coffee cans, chimney flues, piles of old tires, rusted-out wheelbarrows, red wagons, half whiskey barrels, drain pipes, or washtubs—all have their special appeal. Remember that old adage: What is one man's junk is another man's treasure. Search your shed or garage for possible items to use. Salvage yards offer endless possibilities for recycled materials that can be used to create unusual containers. It's easy to bring to life a rusted-out sink by planting it with a batch of cheery nasturtiums that will tumble over the edge. Or try filling a galvanized washtub with fall-blooming chrysanthemums. Just remember that whatever recycled material you decide to use, there must be a way for water to drain out the bottom.

POTS ON THE MOVE: RELOCATING YOUR CONTAINERS

Plant stands with wheels make moving effortless.

One of the advantages of gardening in containers is the flexibility offered by being able to continually rearrange. This is useful in a land of climate extremes; you can move your pots in response to frost or to sun and heat orientation. Small pots and those made of lightweight materials such as plastic or fiberglass don't present much of a problem when the urge to rearrange strikes. A group of small containers may be placed in a wheelbarrow or wagon and carted around to different locations, or individual small pots can simply be hand-carried to new locations. But very large, heavy containers present more of a challenge.

In an ideal world, it would make sense to place large containers in their permanent locations before you plant them the first time. However, we all know about those occasional compulsions to try something new or more artistic.

A metal hand truck or dolly is useful for moving big pots. For safety's sake, secure the container to the dolly with rope. You can also slide pots around by placing an old rug or piece of cardboard underneath. Some large containers can be tipped on edge and rotated into the new location; however, pots must be round for this to be accomplished. Permanent wheel bases are available in various sizes. These raise the containers for improved air circulation as well as make them easier to relocate. If you're trying to move a container up a flight of steps, try using a plywood ramp. You'll need to tie a strong rope around the pot for pulling it up, and this works best with containers that have rims around the top.

It's wise to get some assistance when attempting to move large containers; you don't want to injure yourself or lose your investment. Be sure to move pots *before* watering since wet soil just adds to the weight.

LEFT: Recycle and plant an old wheelbarrow and you can relocate your plants with ease.

The PotLifter

Check www.PotLifter.com for a tool designed specifically to help gardeners relocate heavy containers and move bags of soil mix and even large boulders. The two ends of the PotLifter are fastened around the container to be moved. Two people (one on either side) then lift up on the handles to pick up the object.

ABOVE: Clay scuppers and chimney flues make unusual containers for succulents.

RIGHT: These containers complement the blue bench and its cushions.

CRITERIA FOR POT SELECTION

When you get ready to select containers for your landscape, consider some of the following: Are the height and diameter proportionate to the size of the plant? Will the shape of the pot complement the plant material? In terms of color and texture, what best shows the foliage and/or flowers? Is your style formal, informal, or just plain funky? Is weight a factor? Do you plan to move the container, or will it remain stationary? Does the pot have drainage holes in the bottom, or must you drill your own? Is the container porous or nonporous? Will it hold water or dry out quickly? Remember to match the porosity to the plant type. Finally, do you have budgetary constraints? Some containers can be quite costly and represent a significant financial investment.

Container Shapes

The shape of the pots you choose influences how water moves through the potting soil. Since cacti and succulents require fast drainage, they need containers that facilitate this. Cacti grown in waterlogged soil will rot and die. Tall pots tend to have drier upper soil and wetter lower soil, like a sponge held vertically. In tall pots the water moves more quickly from top to bottom; therefore, they can be watered more frequently without fear of drowning roots at the surface of the pot. Lower, wide pots have more even moisture distribution from the top of the soil surface to the bottom of the pot (like a sponge laid flat) and encourage horizontal rooting, which is the habit of most succulents and cacti. Cacti and succulents can be grown in tall or wide pots, although traditionally cacti and succulent aficionados have favored low, wide pots. For design purposes it is nice to mix tall and short containers when grouping plants together.

This tiny container at the Santa Barbara Botanic Garden is perfect for succulents that don't need frequent watering.

Size Matters

Containers come in many different sizes, ranging from micro to humongous, with many choices in between. Although small pots are easy to move around, allowing for greater flexibility, they can become watering challenges during the summer months—unless planted with cacti or succulents which require little water. As a general rule, larger containers look best from a design standpoint. If you are planting in humongous pots, remember that they will be very heavy so you may wish to avoid planting them with tender plants that might need to be moved to warmer quarters when freezes are predicted. Although there are pot dollies for moving large containers, using a "move-it-once" strategy is probably best. Ideally you can find permanent locations for the big guys.

When it comes to pot selection, size matters just as much as shape. Sculptural plants such as cacti and agaves generally like close quarters and will thrive in pots that are only slightly larger than the plant itself. For these types of plants, you will need to keep transplanting them, or "up potting," until they are close to their mature size. For other plants, such as large woody shrubs or small trees, starting out with a large pot that is able to accommodate the size of the mature plant is desirable.

We offer the following size-descriptive categories for containers:

- Micro: 4–8" in diameter
- Small: 9–17" in diameter
- Medium: 18–23" in diameter
- Large: 24–35" in diameter
- Humongous: 36" plus in diameter

Neutral earth tones look great with bright colors like chartreuse.

Drainage and Drainage Holes

Whether short or tall, all of your containers need drainage holes—no plant will survive long without them. If you purchase pots without drainage holes you can make your own using an electric drill and ceramic drill bit. Before you drill, mark an "X" with masking tape where both the entry and exit holes for the drill bit will be. This is to avoid spalling (breaking off chips) as the drill moves through the pot. To avoid clogging your drainage holes with soil particles, your holes should be a minimum of ¾" in diameter. For large pots, you may need more holes (3–5) to provide adequate drainage. High-fired pottery will require some muscle and patience. Avoid touching the drill bit after drilling—it will be extremely hot!

Once your drainage hole is drilled, you need to think about how to keep soil from washing out the hole. A common misconception is that placing a layer of rocks or pot shards in the bottom of the pot will result in better drainage; in reality, this slows the water movement out of the pot because of the change in soil texture from soil to rocks or shards. To keep your soil mix from washing out the bottom of the pot, you have a couple of options. You can place one loose-fitting rock or single pot shard over the hole as a sort of loose-fitting stopper, or you can place a small square scrap of window screening material over the drainage hole.

POTS ON HIGH

Since good air circulation is important for root development and growth, containers should be raised off the ground or the surface on which they sit. Pot feet, available at nurseries and garden centers, are one way to raise your containers and to ensure good air circulation that will keep roots cooler. Often made out of terra-cotta, pot feet are placed beneath pots, raising them an inch or two from the ground. Some are plain and unadorned; others are quite decorative and come in various animal shapes. Place a mini-

LEFT: Place an inverted pot under your planted container to increase air circulation.

BELOW: This container's "feet" raise it off the ground just slightly, but it's enough to allow for the movement of air.

mum of three under each container; larger pots may require four. Some containers come with their own built-in feet. Plant stands are also available, and some come with wheels, allowing you to rearrange your pots with ease.

If you don't want to spend the money or don't like the look of pot feet or plant stands, there are other alternatives: bricks or trivets work just fine. You can also upend other pots and place them underneath. Using inverted containers can add a decorative touch as well as enabling you to achieve varying heights in a container grouping. Metal tables are another way to go, particularly those with mesh that allow for easy drainage.

The height attained by the placement of the lower pot allows elephant's food (*Portulacaria afra*) to trail freely.

COLLECTION SAUCERS

Although you might be tempted to use collection saucers under your containers in order to avoid water stains, it is not recommended. In general, plant roots do not like to sit in water, and saucers also cut off air circulation to the plants. Saucers with standing water also serve as potential habitat for mosquito larvae. Raising your containers lessens the possibility of permanent discoloration—the result of excessive salt build-up that comes from frequent watering. By raising pots, water is not trapped beneath, and you can hose down the area to avoid stains.

POT TEMPERATURE

If you have ever tried to lift an empty dark-colored, glazed pot onto a nursery cart on a summer afternoon, you know how hot pottery can get. A glazed pot in full sun on a June day may require gloves just to touch it. High soil temperatures can seriously damage the roots of plants in containers—even cacti don't like it. A recent study found that plants grown in black nursery pots have little to no root growth on their south and west sides, the sides that are exposed to full sun, and that their soil temperatures can climb to 120 degrees F. This is something to keep in mind when shopping for a pot—dark colors and full sun equal a very hot vessel. This is particularly true for high-fired glazed pottery from Vietnam and China. It is also true of cast iron and other metal containers. Here are several strategies for dealing with this problem:

- Choose light-colored containers—the lighter the color, the less likely you are to get heat buildup problems.
- Use glazed and cast iron pots only in locations protected from intense afternoon sun.
- Insulate glazed and cast iron pots internally with foam (either in rolls or spray; see "Cool Your Pots" sidebar on page 31).

Grouping similarly colored pots and plants together enhances their impact.

- If the pot must be placed in a very hot location, choose a light color, insulate the interior of the pot, and select only the toughest plant material (e.g., cacti and succulents that are adapted to full sun and reflected heat).

Cool Your Pots

Here are three insulation techniques to keep your pots cooler. When insulating containers, remember that you want to focus on the sides of the pot, taking special care not to clog the drainage holes in the bottom of the pot. In most cases, you don't really need to insulate the bottom of the pot anyway.

Expanding Foam Sealants

Expanding foam is a product used to fill wall cavities and the gaps around newly installed windows and doors. Manufacturers make both low and high expansivity sealants, and for insulating pots you want the lower expansivity type (labeled for windows and doors rather than for wall cavities). One brand of window and door foam is Dow Chemical's "Great Stuff Window and Door Sealant." When sealing a container, start at the bottom and work your way up the sides in a spiral pattern, as if you were making a soft-serve ice cream cone with a hollow center. Because the foam expands, make sure that your pot is large enough to accommodate the foam, potting soil, and root ball of your plant. Expanding foam is not recommended for containers in which you are growing edible plants.

Foil-backed Bubble Wrap Insulation

This type of insulation is perfect for large cylindrical metal pots, where using large quantities of expanding foam sealant would prove too expensive. It works by creating a thermal break between the hot sides of a container and the root ball. The foil backing reflects as much as 97 percent of the radiant energy that strikes the surface of the pot. It works particularly well in recycled objects, such as old 55-gallon steel drums that have been converted to plant containers. Foil-backed bubble wrap type insulation comes in rolls that can be cut to size with scissors. One brand that is good is Reflectix small project rolls, which come in rolls that are 24" wide and 10' long.

Styrofoam Cups

For small pots with little room for bulky insulation, using regular Styrofoam cups as a thermal break can work well, particularly on those that echo the shape of the cup (pots with tapering sides). Simply cut the bottom off the cup, slit open the side, and insert the cup into your pot. If the cup is not large enough to make it clear around the interior circumference of the pot, cut a section of another cup to fill the gap. Take care to trim the Styrofoam below the rim of the pot so that the unsightly white Styrofoam edge will be covered with soil and/or mulch.

This cream spike agave (*Agave parryi* var. *pattonii* 'Cream Spike') is well staged in a Mike Cone pot.

CHAPTER 2:

Designing with Pots

THERE ARE NO HARD AND FAST RULES when it comes to arranging a group of container plantings, but here are a few suggestions to create order and add zing and vigor to a patio's container arrangement:

- Don't display plants in black plastic nursery pots. These are not made for aesthetics and their utilitarian nature lacks panache on the patio. You'll be surprised at how snappy even the least expensive clay container looks as a replacement for an ugly black plastic pot. Enough said.
- Consolidate pot colors. If you have a mishmash collection of colors and styles that look messy, consider discarding them all and starting fresh with a single unifying color of pot. Even if sizes and styles vary, by choosing one color, or a small number of complementary colors, you will help unite your design and create a harmonious visual motif (also known as rhythm).
- Go eclectic. If you have a large collection of different yet exquisite pots, group them together to show off the fact that they are a collection rather than random purchases. You can also make a diverse pot collection "read" more like a unified

A diverse plant collection of asparagus fern, veggies, and perennials is unified by the use of similarly colored pots.

style by planting a number of similar plants in them (e.g., torch cactus species or agave species).

- Choose an interesting pot. This could be a recycled 55-gallon steel drum, an old pickup truck bed, or a coffee can with attractive graphics. If the pot is compelling, you are halfway there.

MONOPOTTING AND STAGING SPECIMEN PLANTS

Putting just one pumped-up muscular plant in a pot rather than a multi-plant assortment is a design trend called monopotting. Its basic tenet is that pots need not be crammed with countless species of hangers-on, but rather are better with just one iconic plant. The monopot idea works particularly well in the Southwest, where the number of available eclectic and interesting succulent plants is endless. As you grow these plants, over time you will most likely end up with some exceptional individuals that deserve to be highlighted by themselves. We call these plants "specimens," and highlighting them in a carefully selected container is a process that serious cactus and succulent collectors call "staging." Most cactus and succulent societies have shows where they judge both the quality of the specimen plants as well as their presentation. Larry Grammer, a cactus and succulent staging pro from California Cactus Center in Pasadena, offers the following advice on staging:

- Remember that the plant is usually the number-one element. You want to select containers that show off the plant's best characteristics rather than detracting from them.
- Design the arrangement with a viewing angle in mind. Pick the "front" or best side of the plant. Do the same thing with the pot, especially with handmade pots. Potting on a lazy Susan can help with determining best angles.
- Agaves and other rosette-formed plants often lean in nature. In pots, these species look smart when they lean toward the viewer. You can use large rocks to brace them up in the pot.
- Most cacti and succulents look good and thrive in shallow pots. If the container you are transplanting into is more shallow than the pot you are transplanting from (out of), you can raise the root ball and place stones around it; this helps keep some moisture available to the plant roots since large rocks store water.
- If the pot is considerably larger than the plant, use rocks around the circumference to fill in.
- As top dressing, small uniform pebbles, like those found on anthills, make an excellent and tidy-looking surface between the plant and larger rocks.

ABOVE: Strongly shaped plants like this 'Blue Glow' agave can stand on their own.

BELOW: A pair of 'Macho Mocha' mangave plants serve as bookends for lounge chairs.

Leafy Plant Design Tip

If you are trying to fill an attractive container with a variety of leafy plants, the following tip almost always creates something interesting. Choose three different types of plants: something tall, something tufty, and something that drapes. For example, if you were planning a pot of cool-season growers, you could plant hollyhocks (tall), ornamental kale (tufty), and nasturtiums (draping). Of course, you may need more than one of each of these to make the pot look full, and you'll also want to choose colors that work together, but this little rule is often a good place to start.

ABOVE: A grid of 16 baseball plants creates geometric interest.

BELOW: This checkerboard pattern alternates kitchen tiles with *Notocactus leninghausii.*

CONTEMPORARY STAGING

In traditional cactus and succulent staging, plants and rocks are arranged in containers in a naturalistic fashion that might recall the plants' native range or habitat. In contemporary staging, plants are used in a more rhythmic and sculptural way to create a kind of living, potted work of modern art. Following are a few techniques for contemporary staging using sculptural plants:

1 Create grids of plants in square pots or concentric circles in round pots. Good plant candidates for these are baseball plant (*Euphorbia obesa*) and Arizona rainbow hedgehog cactus (*Echinocereus rigidissimus*).

2 Use creative propagation techniques. For plants such as prickly pear that root easily from leaf cuttings, arrange the cuttings in pots to form geometric patterns. Good candidates for this treatment include tuxedo spine prickly pear (*Opuntia violacea macrocentra*) and milk-chocolate spine prickly pear (*Opuntia violacea gosseliniana*).

3 Use masses of white-spined hairy cactus, such as snow pole (*Cleistocactus strausii*) and Old Man of the Andes (*Oreocereus celsianus*) with contrasting top dressings.

4 Use unusual top dressing materials such as crushed or polished glass or black pebbles. Additionally, strips of colored tile can be used to separate two different species of plants.

POT PLACEMENT IDEAS

Entry Areas

If there is room, and especially if an entry area is symmetrical, front doors can be flanked with two matching pots with identical plants. In asymmetrical entryways, try one large pot with a tall plant placed on whichever side of the doorway affords the most room. In general, a taller plant will compete better with the strong vertical lines of the door. For shady entry areas, you'll need to use plants that can withstand the low light levels—try twin-flowered agave (*Agave geminiflora*), spider agave (*Agave bracteosa*), or palma de la virgen (*Dioon edule*), to name a few.

Narrow Walkways

Using a line of matching pots and plants along an outdoor hall or passageway is a good and effective way to provide interest and help move people through a space.

Porch Support Posts

Porch support posts can be dressed up, or minimized, by clustering a group of three pots (one large, one medium, and one small) around each post. These look best if all of the pots are of the same color but of different heights.

Corners

In corners, try placing a trio of pots (small, medium, and large) with the tallest pot at the back of the corner. Plants with some height, such as *Adenium* and *Pachypodium* spp., often look good in the tallest pot in a corner.

ABOVE: Sixteen cut pads of purple prickly pear make for an interesting container arrangement.

BELOW: Willow-green concrete planters planted with slipper plant flank this entry gate.

Stairways

If you have a staircase wide enough to allow it, lining one side of the stairs (preferably the side without a stair rail) with a series of matching pots and plants lends rhythm to the architecture.

RIGHT: Golden barrels in cobalt-blue pots lead the eye upward.

BELOW: An arty pot placed in a bed of succulents adds interest.

LEFT: Mexican tree ocotillo potted in a planting area brings a wild rhythm beside a walkway.

BELOW: The unusual boojum tree deserves a special spot where its singular beauty can be admired.

In Planted Areas

In landscaped areas of the garden, there are two interesting approaches. One is to fit a particularly attractive urn-shaped pot, empty, into a composition of ornamental grasses or beneath the canopy of a tree. Another strategy is to partially bury a pot in a way that leaves a portion of the lip of the pot below grade. In the pot, you can plant trailing plants (such as ice plant) that will trail out of the container. If you choose this method, make sure that the lowest portion of the pot drains. You can also do this with broken pots.

In Trees

In large desert trees that often have more than one trunk, pots can sometimes be balanced in the crotch of two branches. Or, plants such as rat-tail cactus and burro's tail can be used as hanging baskets in a tree. Festooning a tree with multiple succulent hanging baskets adds another layer of interest to the tree and recalls Mexican courtyards where trees are sometimes laden with climbing cacti.

Around Pools

If space is available, try placing three large matching pots behind the back side of the pool where they are visible from the house and look like part of the overall design of the pool area. If deck chairs are part of the view, they can be bookended with two large pots.

POTTERY ARTIST: MIKE CONE

Calling Mike Cone's distinctive vessels otherworldly is appropriate because they look as though they were either forged by demons in Middle-earth or collected by the Mars Lander. Considering that Mike's early work consisted of ceramic monsters, his more recent wildly stylized pots should come as no surprise.

Mike Cone's fantastically shaped pots are a good match for sculptural plants.

A San Francisco Bay Area native, Mike Cone has been working with clay since he was 14 when he began hanging around a San Francisco studio until the owner decided to pay him to pour molds. Years later, after a move to the Arizona desert to escape long commutes, Cone's artistic focus turned to the botanical: "I began making flower pots when I couldn't find anything I liked locally," says Cone, "I wanted to find something functional I could use in gardens."

Cone's pots are entirely hand-built. His pinch pots "are based on one of the first things you learn in ceramics: to stick your finger in a ball of clay then shape it like a pie-crust through pinching." Although Cone uses commercial glazes, he tweaks them to achieve richer colors, "I use low-fire glazes and I burn them to get different effects." Since all of his pots are high-fired, they are built for long life in the garden.

Although his pots border on the fantastic, they are not without pattern and repetition. Using found objects and handmade clay stamps, Cone imprints patterns on his pots. His favorite stamping tools include deer antlers, fish bones, a stamp adapted from a floral button, and dog bones. "I'm a modern fanatic, and more than anything, I like simple repeated designs. I moved to the desert and adopted a clean sparse desert aesthetic. I'm basically fighting Southwest kitsch." Cone's favorite pot, an earthy brown wavy rectangle imprinted with celadon rectangles, is demure compared to some of his brighter colors: "I don't mind bold color, but I prefer the natural clay. With their strong shapes, my pots often don't require the embellishment of color."

POTTERY ARTIST: JAN BELL

Jan Bell makes pots whose textures are inspired by nature. "When I'm searching for pot ideas, I like going to the trees and camping near them. This is my way of communing with the landscape." In fact, Bell's work requires her to head out into nature because the texture of her pots is taken directly from the bark of trees. Some of her favorites include the inner layers of ironwood bark on trees that may have been dead for 100 years. She brings her clay right to the site and lays it on the back, creating an impression that she fashions into a pot. In addition to ironwood trees, Bell has used the bark of Arizona cypress from Chiricahua National Monument for their strong texture. She began creating bark impressions when she slapped a piece of clay on the trunk of a California fan palm, saw the texture and said, "Wow!" These days, Bell's organic yet abstract designs are highly sought after. She thinks that on some level they remind people of planting a plant in the trunk of a tree.

LEFT: An array of potted succulents at the Arizona-Sonora Desert Museum.

CHAPTER 3:

Plants

SCULPTURAL PLANTS

In the category of sculptural plants, we include cacti, succulents, a few palms, and some oddities that are well adapted to container culture. Sculptural plants are characterized by bold silhouettes, drought tolerance, and general evergreen form. Cacti and succulents, and a variety of other plants also known as sculptural plants, are at the very heart of the desert container garden. Because these plants have evolved mechanisms to cope with extreme heat and drought, they should be the first choice for gardeners seeking high-impact, low-care pots. For the frequent traveler, growing potted herbs or annual flowers can be hopeless without employing someone to water while you are away. This is one of the great challenges of container gardening during the dry summer months (especially May and June) in the Southwest. Since the water needs of potted leafy plants are very high during the hot season, they may not be the best choice for some gardeners, particularly those who are here only for part of the year. Substituting bold cacti and succulents (which are grouped together here as "sculptural plants") for flowers (flowering plants) is also an excellent way to

ABOVE: Differently shaped, glazed blue containers show off sculptural plants.

BELOW RIGHT: A pair of baseball plants.

provide a "sense of place" to the Southwest garden, as well as a way to reduce the amount of watering and care required to keep your containers in top shape. Many of the selections listed in this chapter (particularly the cacti) will easily survive (and in some cases prefer) two weeks between waterings.

Special Culture for Sculptural Plants

WATERING CACTI AND SUCCULENTS The question, "How often do I water?" is a common one when it comes to containerized cacti and succulents. The answer is basically: when the soil is almost dry. A good schedule to begin with is once per week in the summer, and once per month in the winter. Of course, this needs to be adapted to each plant's specific situation. The amount of water a plant uses is related to the size and type of pot it's in, the soil mix, sun and wind exposure, and the growth rate of the species. It should also be noted that more frequent watering during a plant's growing season results in faster growth. In general, higher light levels and temperatures, combined with lower humidity, call for more frequent watering.

FERTILIZER FOR CACTI AND SUCCULENTS Most cacti and succulents come from parts of the world with poor mineralized soils and therefore generally don't require much in the way of fertilization. However, because these plants often grow at a slow rate, most hobby gardeners and nearly all commercial cactus and succulent growers "push" their plants with fertilizer. The key thing to remember when it comes to fertilization is that too

little is better than too much and you should fertilize a plant only during its growing season. For example, if you were fertilizing Mexican fencepost cactus, a summer grower, you would not want to feed it after Labor Day—doing so could result in tender new growth that could be damaged by fall frosts. You also want a fertilizer without too much nitrogen (the first number on fertilizer labels). Too much nitrogen can result in weak growth.

There are three options for cactus and succulent fertilizer:

1 Buy a prepackaged "Cactus and Succulent" fertilizer. These are typically in liquid form and have a nitrogen, phosphorus, and potassium (NPK) analysis that is usually something like 2-7-7.

2 Use a regular fertilizer and apply one-half or one-quarter the amount the label recommends for other plants.

3 Use a slow-release fertilizer that you mix into your potting soil, still at one-half or one quarter the amount the label recommends for other plants.

ALOE WATERING: GETTING YOUR AFRICAN PLANTS THROUGH THE SUMMER Some specific plant groups require a little planning to keep them healthy. One of these groups is the aloes. Although aloes grow almost effortlessly fall through spring, come summer, you need to pay some attention to how you water them. Aloes dislike high summer temperatures accompanied by high humidity. Since aloes are winter growers whose roots close up shop in the summer, they can rot out if too much moisture is retained around their roots during the hot season. During the summer months, aloes should be watered at the same frequency but with less water. Think of giving them a brisk sprinkle rather than a deep soak. This goes against the conventional watering wisdom that says to water until water flows out of the container's drainage hole, but it is effective for aloes. Another strategy is to plant other summer growing plants such as silver pony-foot (*Dichondra argentea*) or rain lilies (*Zephyranthes* spp.) around your aloes which will take up the extra moisture and keep the aloe roots firm and rot-free.

WATERING AGAVES, BEAR GRASSES, HESPERALOES, AND YUCCAS The woody lilies, as this group of plants is sometimes known, are extremely durable but are generally not as quite as drought tolerant as true cacti. Therefore, they should be watered a bit more. For these plants, consider a schedule of twice per week in summer, and twice per month in winter. As discussed previously, this schedule will need to be adapted to the plant's specific situation and local weather.

ABOVE: Spider agave is a switch hitter whose leaves make beautiful shadows in the afternoon light.

BELOW RIGHT: Baja "Punk Rock Hairdo" cacti in painted zinc pots make up an address number.

Agaves, Bear Grasses, Hesperaloes, and Yuccas

Plants in this group all have stems that spring from a central rosette—some look like stars, others like fountains. This group includes some of the most dramatic and striking plants for desert landscapes and are highly sought after by collectors and aficionados. One could easily build an entire container garden around a collection of different agaves or yuccas. Because of advances in clonal propagation technology, new and highly prized species that were found only in exclusive collections are now available to all interested parties via the Internet. An example of one of these boutique plants now available to the masses is 'Blue Glow' agave—a striking plant with blue-green leaves and a semi-transparent cordovan-colored edge that glows when it is backlit.

In terms of design, agave species often look their best when they are potted singly. They are so bold that isolating just one plant in a pot seems appropriate (see "Monopotting and Staging Specimen Plants" on page 36).

Barrel Cacti

Easy to grow and striking in pots, some type of barrel cactus should be part of every container garden in the Southwest. Although the golden barrel is by far the most popular plant in this group, a different take on potted barrels can be achieved by planting some of the red-spined varieties. This is best accomplished by using fire barrels, Mexican hairy

barrels, or Baja fire barrels. These plants have candy-apple red spines and during the winter their flesh turns red as well. For a conversation piece, the Baja "Punk Rock Hairdo" barrel fits the bill. Its remarkably long red spines give it a "Sid Vicious meets Sputnik" look. The list on pages 57–58 contains other garden-worthy species that anyone who catches the barrel bug will be sure to want to include in their collection.

Hedgehogs and Torch Cacti

With their relatively short stature, spiny furred arms, and brilliant oversized flowers, hedgehogs and torch cacti make excellent container specimens. Hedgehogs are particularly attractive in trough-style planters. A collection of some of the many hybrids of torch cacti looks smart when grouped together. A couple of the particularly handsome flowering torch cacti are 'Epic' and 'Volcano Sunrise,' although the number of new hybrids seems to grow daily.

Fendler's hedgehog (*Echinocereus fendleri*) is excellent in long shallow planters.

Hedgehogs in pots look especially handsome when they are lined up in pots along the tops of masonry benches or low walls. The golden hedgehog looks particularly glowing when it is positioned in a spot where the early or late sun can backlight its blonde needles. Some of the smaller varieties, such as the Arizona rainbow hedgehog cactus, can be planted in a grid or concentric circles (a grid in a square pot or circles in a round pot) for an eye-catching modern look.

Columnar Cacti

Columnar cacti seem to get all of the attention in popular culture. The anthropomorphic form of plants such as saguaros and other columnar species make them the subjects of frequent caricatures for cartoonists and ad men. The image of a cowboy-hat-wearing saguaro with a friendly upturned arm and "howdy" caption has become an iconic, if kitschy, symbol of the Southwest. In pots, these plants are quite literally "pillars" of the garden. Their often fluted columns are exceptionally handsome marking entryways or tucked up against walls where they draw the eye upward. The largest plants in the list on pages 58–59 often look best when they are placed (in a nice container) into part of the garden surrounded by other vegetation rather than wedged onto a patio or porch. Wherever you place them, be sure to leave enough room for the eye-catching columns to grow into the large dignified plants that is their destiny. Along with ocotillos and yuccas, columnar cacti can also be used as a kind of scaffolding for small vines to climb on. In nature, this happens without human help; near Loreto Bay in Baja California Sur, Mexico, it is common to find organ pipe cacti with queen's wreath vine rambling over and around its stems. With the right vines and a little bit of training (for the vines) you can create this cool layered effect with your potted columnar cactus.

ABOVE: Columnar cacti like Argentine saguaro (*Echinopsis terscheckii*) look great on columnar pedestals.

Mickey Mouse Plants

With leaves the shape of a certain Disney character's ears, prickly pear cacti are popular landscape plants in the arid Southwest. It is less common to find them used in pots. The

RIGHT: Purple prickly pear is contained in a raised steel bed.

For the Birds

Ocotillo bloom.

From a bird's perspective, it's tough to beat the tasty, pulpy fruits of Engelmann's prickly pear (*Opuntia engelmannii*). The purple-red fruits ripen in late summer and are feasted upon by many species of birds, including finches, thrashers, doves, woodpeckers, and even hummingbirds. Small mammals relish them as well.

The early spring blooms of various aloes delight hummingbirds.

The arching branches of ocotillo (*Fouquieria splendens*) provide ideal perching spots for birds. Flame-colored blooms in spring attract orioles, verdins, and hummers.

Red hesperaloe (*Hesperaloe parviflora*) is tougher than nails and blooms all summer long, attracting hummingbirds and verdins.

The tall flower spikes of giant hesperaloe (*Hesperaloe funifera*) make useful perches for delivering songs, courtship displays, or simply for surveying the surrounding landscape. White flowers attract insects and the birds that feed on them.

Southwest coral bean (*Erythrina flabelliformis*), while not much to look at for part of the year, rewards us with brilliant scarlet tubular flowers in late spring and hummingbirds love them.

The upright semi-succulent stems of slipper plant (*Pedilanthus macrocarpus*) sport red flowers in late winter/spring as well as in late summer/fall and draw hummingbirds.

Aloe ferox flowers.

species in the list on page 59 are small enough for container culture and look particularly handsome when they are planted in pots and strategically placed next to in-ground desert shrubs such as creosote and Mormon tea. Consult Chapter 2, "Designing with Pots," for more ideas (page 35).

Ocotillo

Big burly plants in the *Fouquieria* genus are not often considered as suitable for container plantings, but they should be! At the Arizona-Sonora Desert Museum, workers have expertly planted Mexican tree ocotillo in shallow pots with a top dressing of large

RIGHT: A very large concrete pot has sufficient bulk to hold an ocotillo at the Las Vegas Springs Preserve.

chunky rocks that highlights the texture of the trunk. Since ocotillos grow and shed their leaves several times each year in response to rain and drought, they make a dynamic and changing sculptural piece in the garden. Even without leaves, the zigzag, thorned lightning of their branches is eye-catching.

Because they are indeed thorny, containerized ocotillo plants are best set back some distance from walkways and other high traffic areas. Their relatively narrow width makes them a logical choice for a hot narrow spot against a wall. This produces a bonus effect: zigzag shadows.

BELOW: A strange plant like this gorilla's armpit is housed in a suitably strange Mike Cone pot.

Intriguingly Weird Plants

These "weird" plants are species that don't fit neatly into any of the other categories listed in this book. Since these plants are unusual and tend to be conversation pieces, it's a good idea to put them where they will get noticed. The smallest look good on table tops, while larger specimens might be placed in the corners of patios.

You can also get good results by clustering weird plants together in containers. For example, a group of three to five bishop's caps in a low bowl with rock top dressing makes for distinctive container planting.

Amazing Aloes

Aloes are the winter-growing African counterparts to agaves. Because they are some of the first plants to bloom in spring, they are highly valued as potted specimens. As winter growers, they like the winter sun and some shade in the summer. As mentioned in the watering section, be careful not to rot aloe roots in the summer. A south-facing patio, where plants can bask in the winter sun (when it is at a low angle) and receive shade in the summer, is the ideal location. Since many aloes are sensitive to frost, you will need to cover them or pull them under an awning to protect them on cold desert nights. (None are hardy at temperatures much below 15 degrees F.) This is especially true once plants begin pushing up their candelabra-like bloom stalks: if bloom stalks freeze, the plant will not bloom again until the following year. Because of their frost sensitivity, aloes are well suited to containers that can be moved and positioned for maximum warmth on frosty nights.

ABOVE: 'Blue Elf' aloe (*Aloe* x 'Blue Elf') blooms January through April and is relatively cold-tolerant.

Palms and Cycads

For evoking that lush Mexican hacienda look on your patio, nothing beats the luxuriant leaves of palms. Many make great container plants, but the species in the list on page 62 (with some similarly shaped cycads thrown in) are smaller, slower growing, and well

LEFT: Handsome *Dioons* lend a tropical feel.

adapted to pot culture. When selecting a container for your palms, choose one that is taller than it is wide with good drainage holes and use a fast-draining soil mix. Since palms are warm-season growers, you can fertilize them with specific "palm" fertilizers beginning in May. These fertilizers usually have high nitrogen and potassium numbers but relatively low phosphorus numbers: typically labels would have NPK numbers such as 12-4-12.

Sexy Spurges

The genus *Euphorbia* is such a large family of plants that there is room for relatives as diverse as the giant candelabra tree (*Euphorbia ingens*), which in its native Swaziland is a fast-growing 50-foot-tall tree, and the familiar poinsettia (*Euphorbia pulcherima*), our well-known holiday plant from Mexico. With over 8,000 species ranging in size from annual wildflowers to large trees, it's hard to know where a gardener should begin with this group of plants. All *Euphorbias* contain a milky sap (which some people are allergic to), and many come from the African continent. The following are great choices for containers:

- **Baseball Plant** (*Euphorbia obesa*) This almost unnaturally round, fat plant is so spherical and bald that it has been compared to a stone, a sea urchin and, of course, its namesake—the baseball. It is hard to imagine a plant any more globe-like. The plant ranges from a sage-green to grey-green in color and with a stout appearance that explains the species half of its scientific name: *obesa* is Latin for "plump" or "obese." The plant's rotund profile is enhanced by latitudinal bands that recall stretch marks on a very pregnant woman's belly. The plant appears to barely be able to contain its own girth. Prized by gardeners around the globe for its unusual shape, it makes a very fine potted plant in shallow, brightly glazed containers.
- **Candelilla** (*Euphorbia antisyphilitica*) Of the euphorbias listed here, candelilla is unquestionably the toughest. Hailing from the thin calcareous soils of West Texas and New Mexico, it is impervious to soil type and drought and will even withstand years of root-bound neglect in a pot. Not only is it tough, it's also not hard on the eyes. Like a dwarf slipper plant, candelilla bears stems which rise up like little blue-gray pencils and are both handsome and architectural. The plant's common name (*candelilla* is Spanish for "small candle") comes from the fact that the plant can be rendered into a wax. Following spring and summer rains, candelilla produces clusters of small pink flowers up and down its stems. Since candelilla reaches a height of only 18 inches and is usually less than 2 feet wide, it is perfect for small containers.

- **Crown of Thorns** (*Euphorbia milii*) Often compared to a big thorny octopus, the branches of the crown of thorns undulate and curve like tentacles tipped with fire-red suction cups. The little cup-shaped bracts are showy indeed and have encouraged growers to breed this plant for both bract color and size. In most of the Southwest, crown of thorns is best confined to areas beneath covered patios because of its lack of cold and sun tolerance; when sited under a covered porch it is quite resilient. At Tucson Botanical Gardens, a venerable specimen nestled under a north-facing porch produces a dazzling summer show of red bracts and lives happily with little care.
- **Medusa's Head** *(Euphorbia esulenta)* Widely appreciated for its serpentine appearance, Medusa's head is a fine choice for containers. Although the stems do appear vaguely snakelike, the plant appears more like a well-behaved rosette than a twisting wig of vipers. Storing water in a large underground caudex, Medusa's head is very water thrifty; it may, however, need some protection from hard frosts. In contrast to Moroccan mound, Medusa's head has medium-green, rather than gray or silver, serpentine branches.
- **Moroccan Mound** (*Euphorbia resinifera*) If the thought of cobalt blue Marrakech courtyards jammed with strange succulents sets your heart racing, the Moroccan mound is a plant for you. True to its name, the Moroccan mound is nothing if not symmetrical and its beautiful pale green, four-sided arms contrast nicely with brightly colored walls. Moroccan mound produces a line of small chartreuse bracts in late spring. Because of its symmetrical shape, it is a smart choice for pots in both contemporary and formal gardens.

SCULPTURAL PLANT CHARTS

Asterisks indicate plants that tolerate shade.

AGAVES, BEAR GRASSES, HESPERALOES, AND YUCCAS

PLANT NAME	MATURE HEIGHT X WIDTH	COLD HARDINESS (DEGREES F)	POT SIZE NEEDED	CONTAINER DESIGN NOTES
Artichoke Agave (*Agave parryi* var. *truncata*)	3' x 3'	10	Medium to Large	Highly ornamental. Plant in paired pots to flank entryways.
Banana Yucca (*Yucca baccata*)	4' x 6'	–20	Medium	Wonderful filaments on the leaf margins. Great paired with low-growing yellow dot (*Wedelia trilobata*).
Beaked Yucca* (*Yucca rostrata*)	10' x 4'	–20	Large to Humongous	Dramatic blue trunk-forming yucca.
Bear Grass* (*Nolina microcarpa*)	5' x 7'	–10	Medium to Large	In pots, the width is constrained. No sharp points.
Bell-flowered Hesperaloe (*Hesperaloe campanulata*)	3' x 3'	10	Medium	Light pink hummingbird-attracting flowers. Withstands harsh conditions.
'Blue Glow' Agave (*Agave attenuata* x *ocahui* 'Blue Glow')	2–3' x 2–3'	15	Medium	Resistant to cold and most critters.
Butterfly Agave* (*Agave potatorum*)	2' x 2'	25	Medium	Exceptionally handsome silver plant with twisted reddish spines.
Desert Agave (*Agave deserti*)	1.5' x 2'	15	Medium	A nice, small, underused agave.
Durango Delight Agave (*Agave schidigera* 'Durango Delight')	2' x 2'	15	Small to Medium	Handsome white-streaked leaves have white filaments.
Giant Hesperaloe (*Hesperaloe funifera*)	6' x 6'	–10	Medium to Large	Big deep-green sword-like leaves.
Jet-Tipped Agave* (*Agave macroacantha*)	2' x 2'	25	Small to Medium	Black spines and lots of offsets.
Mescal Ceniza (*Agave colorata*)	3–4' x 3–4'	15	Medium	Looks like it was dusted with powdered sugar.
Ocahui (*Agave ocahui*)	2' x 3'	15	Small to Medium	Deep green solitary rosette, takes reflected heat.

(Agaves, Bear Grasses, Hesperaloes, and Yuccas continued)

PLANT NAME	MATURE HEIGHT X WIDTH	COLD HARDINESS (DEGREES F)	POT SIZE NEEDED	CONTAINER DESIGN NOTES
Octopus Agave* (*Agave vilmoriniana*)	3' x 3'	20	Medium to Large	Sexy recurving form. Available in a variegated form called 'Stained Glass.'
Pale-leaf Yucca* (*Yucca pallida*)	1–2' x 1–3'	–10	Small to Medium	Non-trunk-forming with silver leaves; looks good with 'Silver Falls' dichondra (*Dichondra argentea* 'Silver Falls').
Parry's Agave (*Agave parryi*)	2' x 3'	–20	Medium to Large	Über cold-hardy and handsome.
Queen Victoria Agave (*Agave victoriae-reginae*)	1.5' x 1.5'	10	Small to Medium	Highly sought after. White markings.
Red Hesperaloe (*Hesperaloe parviflora*)	3' x 3'	–20	Medium	Stalwart and oft used, with showy red-pink bloom stalks.
Spider Agave* (*Agave bracteosa*)	1–2' x 1–2'	10	Small to Medium	Native to canyons; likes shade or sun.
Twin-flowered Agave* (*Agave geminiflora*)	3' x 3'	15	Small to Medium	Deep green straw-shaped leaves.
Twisted Yucca* (*Yucca rupicola*)	2' x 2–3'	–10	Small to Medium	Trunkless with medium green corkscrew leaves.
Whale's Tongue Agave* (*Agave ovatifolia*)	3' x 4'	0	Medium to Large	Huge wide leaves; attractive form.

BARRELS

PLANT NAME	MATURE HEIGHT X WIDTH	COLD HARDINESS (DEGREES F)	POT SIZE NEEDED	CONTAINER DESIGN NOTES
Baja Fire Barrel (*Ferocactus gracilis* var. *coloratus*)	3' x 1'	15	Small to Medium	Deep red gracefully curved spines and red flowers.
Baja "Punk Rock Hairdo" Barrel Cactus (*Ferocactus rectispinus*)	3' x 1'	15	Small to Medium	Extremely long, elegant red spines. Use chunky rocks as top dressing.
Fire Barrel (*Ferocactus pringlei*)	3' x 1'	15	Small to Medium	Very red spines and winter-red flesh.

(Barrels continued)

PLANT NAME	MATURE HEIGHT X WIDTH	COLD HARDINESS (DEGREES F)	POT SIZE NEEDED	CONTAINER DESIGN NOTES
Fishhook Barrel (*Ferocactus wislizeni*)	5' x 2'	10	Medium to Large	Adorned by a crown of orange flowers followed by yellow fruit.
Golden Barrel (*Echinocactus grusonii*)	3' x 4'	10	Medium to Large	Ubiquitous and handsome en masse. Look for multi-headed specimens for pots.
Mexican Hairy Barrel (*Ferocactus stainsii*)	3' x 1'	18	Small to Medium	Red spines with a mesh of white hairs beneath.

HEDGEHOGS AND TORCH CACTI

PLANT NAME	MATURE HEIGHT X WIDTH	COLD HARDINESS (DEGREES F)	POT SIZE NEEDED	CONTAINER DESIGN NOTES
Arizona Rainbow Hedgehog Cactus (*Echinocereus rigidissimus*)	7' x 0.2'	10	Micro to Medium	Striking red stripes. Try planting them in a grid of 9 or 12 plants in a square pot.
Claret Cup (*Echinocereus triglochidiatus* 'White Sands Strain')	1–2' x 3–5'	0	Medium	The largest and fastest growing claret cup variety.
Golden Hedgehog (*Echinocereus nicholii*)	2' x 3'	15	Small to Medium	Glowing yellow spines.
Strawberry Hedgehog (*Echinocereus engelmannii*)	1'x 2'	10	Small to Medium	Commanding form, magenta flowers, and yummy fruit.
Torch Cactus Hybrids* (*Trichocereus* hybrids)	2' x 5'	10	Small to Medium	Impossibly large showy flowers. There are many hybrids with a wide range of flower colors: from blood red ('Fuente de Sangre') to yellow ('June Noon').

COLUMNAR CACTI

PLANT NAME	MATURE HEIGHT X WIDTH	COLD HARDINESS (DEGREES F)	POT SIZE NEEDED	CONTAINER DESIGN NOTES
Mexican Fencepost (*Pachycereus marginatus*)	15' x 4'	25	Large to Humongous	Classic deep-green column with white pinstripes. Likes extra water.
Night-blooming Cereus (*Cereus hildmannianus*)	15' x 6'	15	Large to Humongous	This is the most common species referred to as "night-blooming cereus," although there are others. Often misidentified as Peruvian cereus.
Old Man of the Andes (*Oreocereus celsianus*)	6' x .5'	15	Medium to Large	A long-haired old dude.

(Columnar Cacti continued)

PLANT NAME	MATURE HEIGHT X WIDTH	COLD HARDINESS (DEGREES F)	POT SIZE NEEDED	CONTAINER DESIGN NOTES
Old Man of Mexico (*Cephalocereus senilis*)	20' x 6'	20	Large to Humongous	Snowy long hair.
Old Man of the Mountain (*Oreocereus trollii*)	2' x 3'	20	Medium to Large	White hair bristling with gold spines.
Organ Pipe Cactus (*Stenocereus thurberi*)	10' x 10'	25	Large to Humongous	Sublime fruit, wonderful form.
Senita (*Lophocereus schottii*)	10' x 10'	20	Large to Humongous	Spectacular mop-top hairiness.
Snow Pole (*Cleistocactus strausii*)	8' x 3'	19	Medium to Large	Pure-white spines with red flowers on the sides.
Totempole Cactus (*Pachycereus schottii* var. *monstrous*)	10' x 10'	20	Medium to Large	Angular melted-candle form without spines.

PRICKLY PEARS

PLANT NAME	MATURE HEIGHT X WIDTH	COLD HARDINESS (DEGREES F)	POT SIZE NEEDED	CONTAINER DESIGN NOTES
Beavertail Prickly Pear (*Opuntia basilaris*)	1' x 3'	10	Small to Medium	Good size for small containers. Hot-pink flowers.
Engelmann's Prickly Pear (*Opuntia engelmannii*)	6' x 10–15'	5	Medium to Large	Bulletproof, with tasty fruits.
Grizzly Bear Prickly Pear (*Opuntia erinacea*)	1' x 3'	0	Small to Medium	Interesting hairy spines.
Milk-chocolate Spine Prickly Pear (*Opuntia violacea gosseliniana*)	1–2' x 2–2.5'	10	Small	A miniature Santa Rita with chocolate-colored spines.
Santa Rita Prickly Pear (*Opuntia violacea santa-rita*)	4' x 4'	10	Medium to Large	Purple winter color.
Tuxedo Spine Prickly Pear (*Opuntia violacea macrocentra*)	1' x 5'	0	Small to Medium	Yellow and red flowers, small stature, purple pads.

OCOTILLO

PLANT NAME	MATURE HEIGHT X WIDTH	COLD HARDINESS (DEGREES F)	POT SIZE NEEDED	CONTAINER DESIGN NOTES
Adam's Tree (*Fouquieria diguetii*)	6–15' x 3–6'	25	Medium to Large	Rare in cultivation.
Boojum Tree (*Fouquieria columnaris*)	60' x 5'	15	Medium to Large (and eventually Humongous)	Plant in the fall; very slow-growing.
Mexican Tree Ocotillo (*Fouquieria macdougalii*)	8' x 6' (potted)	26	Medium to Large	Beefy trunks.
Ocotillo (*Fouquieria splendens*)	12–18' x 6–10'	10	Large to Humongous	Pots must be large and heavy enough to support the plant. Could possibly tolerate colder temperatures depending on provenance.

WEIRD PLANTS

PLANT NAME	MATURE HEIGHT X WIDTH	COLD HARDINESS (DEGREES F)	POT SIZE NEEDED	CONTAINER DESIGN NOTES
Bishop's Cap* (*Astrophytum myriostigma*)	12" x 6"	20	Micro to Small	Wonderfully white and ornamental with no long spines. There is also a green form (*Astrophytum myriostigma* f. *nudum*). Both have yellow flowers.
Bulbine (*Bulbine frutescens*)	1' x 2'	15	Small	Green onion-like foliage topped with bright flowers. 'Hallmark' is a compact selection with orange flowers. Works well at the base of agaves or other rosette-shaped plants.
Elephant Tree (*Bursera microphylla*)	12–18' x 12–18'	28	Medium to Large	Makes a fine bonsai specimen. Needs heat and a nearly frost-free area.
Elephant's Food* (*Portulacaria afra*)	3' x 4'	25	Small to Medium	Like a mini-jade plant. Sun or shade.
Gorilla's Armpit (*Calibanus hookeri*)	2–3' x 2–3'	10	Small to Medium	Grass-like plant that grows from a woody caudex. Excellent in tall narrow pots.
'Macho Mocha'* Mangave (*Manfreda* x 'Macho Mocha')	1.5' x 3'	15	Medium	Fleshy leaves with chocolate-purple spots.
Owl's Eyes (*Mammillaria parkinsonii*)	6" x 6–12"	25	Small	Resembles the face of a barn owl.

(Weird Plants continued)

PLANT NAME	MATURE HEIGHT X WIDTH	COLD HARDINESS (DEGREES F)	POT SIZE NEEDED	CONTAINER DESIGN NOTES
Rock Fig (*Ficus petiolaris*)	10–30' x 10–30'	30	Large to Humongous	Great as a bonsai-like specimen with roots trained over rocks.
Slipper Plant* (*Pedilanthus macrocarpus*)	3–4' x 3–4'	25	Medium	Switch hitter: part shade or full sun. Snake-like succulent stems and red flowers.
Southwest Coral Bean (*Erythrina flabelliformis*)	3–6' x 3–6'	15	Medium	Lipstick-red flowers in late spring, early summer.
Star Cactus* (*Astrophytum ornatum*)	2–4' x 6"	20	Small	This close relative to the Bishop's cap has green flesh with white flecks that resembles a star when viewed from above.
Texas Tuberose (*Manfreda maculosa*)	1' x 1–2'	0	Small	A tuberous plant that looks like a little yucca with purple spots.
Twisted Cereus (*Cereus hildmannianus* f. *tortuosus*)	10–15' x 6'	18	Large to Humongous	Its ribs form a nice spiral.

ALOES

PLANT NAME	MATURE HEIGHT X WIDTH	COLD HARDINESS (DEGREES F)	POT SIZE NEEDED	CONTAINER DESIGN NOTES
'Blue Elf' Aloe* (*Aloe* x 'Blue Elf')	1' x 2'	15	Small	Petite with striking blue foliage and coral flowers. Relatively cold-hardy.
Cape Aloe* (*Aloe ferox*)	12' x 5'	25	Medium to Large	Big orange-red flower candelabra in late winter, early spring. Protect from afternoon sun.
Coral Aloe* (*Aloe striata*)	2–3' x 1–2'	25	Small to Medium	Good in entryways or beneath trees.
Kokerbom* (*Aloe dichotoma*)	30' x 20'	23	Large to Humongous	Trunk-forming with interesting foliage pattern. Protect from afternoon sun.
Medicinal Aloe* (*Aloe barbadensis*)	2' x 3'	25	Small to Medium	Fleshy leaves and yellow flowers, used to treat burns. Protect from afternoon sun.
Partridge Breast Aloe* (*Aloe variegata*)	1' x 1'	15	Small	Relatively cold-hardy; dark green leaves with white markings.

PALMS AND CYCADS

PLANT NAME	MATURE HEIGHT X WIDTH	COLD HARDINESS (DEGREES F)	POT SIZE NEEDED	CONTAINER DESIGN NOTES
Dwarf Palmetto* (*Sabal minor*)	5–10' x 5–10'	15	Medium	Attractive underused small palm.
Guadalupe Palm (*Brahea edulis*)	10' x 8'	20	Medium to Large	Great with deer grass beneath.
Mediterranean Fan Palm (*Chamaerops humilis*)	4–8' x 2–6' (depending on pot size)	15	Medium to Large	Has more desirable form and restrained growth in a pot.
Mexican Blue Palm (*Brahea armata*)	25' x 8'	15	Medium to Large	Icy blue foliage; very heat- and cold-tolerant.
Palma de la Virgen* (*Dioon edule*)	2' x 4'	15	Medium to Large	Good underneath desert trees or in shady entryways.
Pygmy Date Palm* (*Phoenix robelenii*)	4–6' x 3–6'	26	Medium	Good in locations protected from cold.
Sago Palm* (*Cycas revoluta*)	2–3' x 2–3'	15	Medium	Good for northern exposures and shady nooks. Leaves will burn in full sun in the low desert.
Sonoran Palmetto* (*Sabal uresana*)	30' x 18'	15	Large to Humongous	Blue-green fronds.
Spiny Dioon* (*Dioon spinulosum*)	6' x 8'	32	Medium to Large	Stunning potted plant with big graceful arching fronds.

SUCCULENT BULBS

The Southwest isn't exactly known for gardens swathed in bulbs, and many a tulip has suffered an ignominious death here. But if you take traditional bulbs out of the picture and replace them with bulbs from South Africa and those from North America, you'll find a good little collection of plants for containers. The following are a few to consider. These are best planted in fall.

- **Blue Dicks** (*Dichelostemma pulchellum*) A small cluster of purple-blue flowers on elegant onion-like stems, blue dicks is a great little bulb native to rocky slopes throughout the Southwest. It can be propagated by seed or bulb (the seed will take three years to come into flower).
- **Cooper's Rain Lily** (*Zephyranthes drummondii*) This strapping white-flowering lily comes up in spring and looks great among grasses and prickly pears from Arizona to Texas.
- **Nerine** (*Nerine filamentosa*) This Eastern Cape wildflower bulb is a summer grower with pretty little, deep-pink flowers with petals that re-curve.

- **Oxblood Lily** (*Rhodophiala bifida*) The deep-red, silver-dollar-sized blooms of the oxblood lily appear in early fall. In the low deserts it appreciates some shade in the summer but is otherwise not particular about growing conditions.
- **Peacock Iris** (*Morea polystacha*) This plant sends up small flowers shaped like little Dutch irises. It blooms on and off for 6–8 weeks from late fall through early spring. It multiplies aggressively, which isn't a problem in a pot.
- **Pink Rain Lily** (*Zephyranthes grandiflora*) A repeat bloomer from summer to fall that loves heat and humidity and produces big deep-pink flowers. Like oxblood lily, it prefers partial shade in the summer.
- **'Prairie Sunset' Rain Lily** (*Zephyranthes* x 'Prairie Sunset') A hybrid lily that keeps its evergreen foliage over the hot summer months and repeatedly sends out apricot flowers.

ABOVE: Rain lily bulbs ready to be potted.

BELOW LEFT: Showy blooms of pink rain lily.

Bulbaceous Plant Partners

Try placing Cooper's rain lily (*Zephyranthes drummondii*) bulbs into a container with perennials such as hummingbird mint (*Agastache*) or dwarf forms of bougainvillea such as 'Rosenka,' 'Torch Glow,' or 'Silhouette' bougainvillea. The grass-like leaves add architectural interest, and showy white flowers (lasting, unfortunately, only one day) bloom in late summer and fall. Other rain lilies (*Zephyranthes* spp.) are appropriate for container planting and do remarkably well when pot-bound. They come in white, pink, and yellow and bloom during the summer monsoon—colorful accents to other plants. Share bulbs with friends.

PERENNIALS FOR POTTED PIZZAZZ

No container garden is complete without the addition of some reliable perennials—plants that live for more than one year. Unlike annuals, which need to be replaced seasonally, well-tended perennials add an air of permanence to container plantings. They are excellent choices for pot gardens in the Southwest for they require less water than annuals, and less fertilizing as well. When perennials are not actively growing, you can cut back on the water significantly, probably about half as much as you would water during the warmer months. And it's simply not necessary to fertilize them over the winter months (November to February). Be sure to choose deeper and wider pots than you would for annuals in order to accommodate larger root systems.

Here are some varieties that are moderate water-users, sport attractive blooms, and boast other desirable characteristics as well:

ABOVE: Autumn sage (*Salvia greggii*).

BELOW: Bloodflower (*Asclepias curassavica*).

- **Autumn Sage** (*Salvia greggii*) A perennial favorite (pardon the pun) in desert gardens, the spring- and fall-blooming red flowers that attract hummingbirds make it very desirable for container culture. It will take some shade and tolerate temperatures as low as 0 degrees F.
- **Bloodflower** (*Asclepias curassavica*) Add fire to your patio with bloodflower, appropriately named for its rich red-orange flowers. This plant enjoys the extra moisture afforded it in a container. Like other members of the milkweed family, it serves as a butterfly larval foodplant for queens and monarchs. Hummingbirds visit the nectar, and verdins and cactus wrens like to use the silken down surrounding the seeds for their nests. Bloodflower blooms recklessly in summer but may freeze to the ground in winter.
- **Blue Mist Flower** (*Ageratum corymbosum*) You can't beat this perennial for attracting queen butterflies. Clusters of light blue flowers contain an alkaloid which males ingest and later release as an aphrodisiac to attract females. Plant in morning sun. Blue mist flower blooms from mid-summer through fall. It doesn't do much during the winter months, so you might want to set out some annuals to carry it over, or move it to a less visible spot. Cut back in late winter/early spring to encourage new growth.
- **Chocolate Flower** (*Berlandiera lyrata*) Who wouldn't want a plant with such an evocative name? This native, low-growing perennial sports yellow and maroon daisy-like flowers that smell like chocolate. Blooms occur spring to fall. Plant in sun or filtered shade, and don't worry about the cold: chocolate flower is hardy to about 5 degrees F.

- **Coral Fountain** (*Russelia equisetiformis*) Dramatic in a roomy container, coral fountain has arching stems and brilliant scarlet tubular flowers that attract hummers. Female quail like to lay their eggs beneath the bending branches. The challenge then becomes how to water without upsetting the birds! Coral fountain appreciates heat but needs to be watered regularly. It can sustain some frost damage but generally recovers quickly.
- **Desert Milkweed** (*Asclepias subulata*) The strong vertical lines of this tough sculptural perennial make it a winner in the container garden. Even in full sun (its preference), it is remarkably drought-tolerant. Creamy yellow flowers are visited by tarantula hawks (*Pepsis* wasps) and other pollinators. Desert milkweed is also a butterfly attractant, serving as a foodplant for the caterpillars of queens and monarchs. Plants grow 3–4 feet high and about 3 feet wide.
- **Dogweed** (*Thymophylla pentachaeta*) This charming native wildflower grows well in containers and looks good with agave and cactus specimens. It prefers full sun and may bloom on and off throughout the year. Dainty sulphur butterflies enjoy the nectar and they also use this plant for laying eggs and feeding their caterpillars. Dogweed reseeds easily and requires little water.
- **Firewheel** (*Gaillardia aristata*) The showy red and yellow, daisy-like flowers of this plant provide cheer for long periods of time—spring through fall, and sometimes

Golden columbine blooms "pop" out behind a deep blue garden bench. Design: Marcia Tatroe.

There are a variety of *Gaillardias* in the nursery trade and most do well in large pots.

into winter as well. This plant doesn't like overhead watering, which can blemish leaves and may contribute to fungal infections. The seed heads are very attractive. Leave them on to attract lesser goldfinches; they relish the seeds.

- **Golden Columbine** (*Aquilegia chrysantha*) In habitat, golden columbine can be found in hanging gardens in canyons where it grows near seeps. In pots a shaded, or at least partly shaded spot, is the way to go. Admittedly, golden columbine does need ample water, but the hummingbirds are fond of its golden yellow flowers with trailing spurs. Hardy to -30 degrees F.
- **Gopher Plant** (*Euphorbia rigida*) For fans of the color chartreuse (and who isn't?), the gopher plant's spring bloom is pure bliss. The yellow-green bracts suspended over silver leaves make for an irresistible combination. Gopher plant is tolerant of heat and can be left alone even on hot southern exposures where it will happily grow, bloom, and reseed. Lengthened stems lend themselves to pot culture as they spill over container edges. Blue-flowering wildflowers like desert bluebells and Goodding's verbena make handsome pairings when sprinkled in the same pot.
- **Hummingbird Mint** (*Agastache* 'Desert Sunrise') This hybrid, a cross between *Agastache cana* and *A. rupestris,* exudes a delightful fragrance. It also blooms nonstop from mid-summer through fall, attracting hummingbirds and their look-alikes, sphinx moths. The flowers are shades of pink, orange, and lavender. Remove old stems in late winter.
- **Indian Mallow** (*Abutilon palmeri*) The fuzzy gray-green leaves of this plant are soft to the touch and look attractive partnered with plants that have contrasting leaf colors.

Yellow-orange blooms adorn the plant in spring and summer followed by attractive persistent seed heads. Indian mallow is hardy to the mid-20s F and appreciates a good trim in late winter.

- **Jerusalem Sage** (*Phlomis fruticosa*) Give this gray-green leafy plant morning sun. It sends up 3–4 foot flower stalks in spring, and the brilliant yellow flowers are stunning. Following bloom, goldfinches flock to the seeds. When the goldfinches are finished, cut back the dead stalks to promote new basal growth. Jerusalem sage likes good drainage and is cold-hardy to the mid-20s F.
- **Lavender** (*Lavandula* spp.) Lavender is tricky here, but appreciates the better drainage afforded by most containers. The heat and humidity of the monsoon can take a toll on these plants. Cut back on the water to avoid root rot. Fernleaf lavender, *L. multifida*, seems to be most successful in coping with the heat/humidity combo. Despite these difficulties, fernleaf lavender is well worth growing for its sweet-scented purple-blue flowers that bloom reliably for three seasons and for the hummingbirds that visit them.
- **Mealy Cup Sage** (*Salvia farinacea*) Although this plant dies back in the winter (try putting a stunning sculpture in the pot to carry it over), it comes back strong in spring and blooms reliably throughout the warm season. Violet-blue flowers occur in dense flower spikes and attract hummingbirds. Remove dead flower spikes to encourage further bloom. Planted containers can be placed in full sun or part shade.

The velvety leaves of Indian mallow make it a good choice in spots where it can be touched.

For the Hummingbirds

Autumn Sage (*Salvia greggii*)
Coral Fountain (*Russelia equisetiformis*)
'Valentine' Emu Bush (*Eremophila maculata* 'Valentine'®)
Hummingbird Mint (*Agastache* 'Desert Sunrise')
Mexican Oregano (*Poliomintha maderensis*)
Scarlet Creeper (*Ipomoea coccinea*)
Shrimp Plant (*Justicia brandegeana*)
Texas Betony (*Stachys coccinea*)
Velvet Honeysuckle (*Dicliptera suberecta*)

For the Butterflies

Queen butterfly on *Ageratum corymbosum* bloom.

Bloodflower (*Asclepias curassavica*): nectar plus larval foodplant for queen and monarch caterpillars
Blue Mist Flower (*Ageratum corymbosum*): nectar plus alkaloids for mating
Desert Milkweed (*Asclepias subulata*): nectar and larval foodplant for queens and monarchs
Dogweed (*Thymophylla pentachaeta*): nectar and larval foodplant for dainty sulphur
Milkweed Vine (*Sarcostemma cynanchoides*): foodplant for queen and monarch caterpillars
Southwestern Pipevine (*Aristolochia watsonii*): foodplant for pipevine swallowtails
Trailing Lantana (*Lantana montevidensis*): nectar for various butterflies

- **Mexican Evening Primrose** (*Oenothera speciosus*) Tough enough to be planted at the base of yucca and agave species, Mexican evening primrose forms a solid carpet of pink blooms in the spring. It will also take partial shade. In the ground it spreads aggressively by rhizomes, which is another reason to keep it contained in a pot.
- **Mexican Oregano** (*Poliomintha maderensis*) One of the best things about this plant is its fragrance; the leaves smell like oregano. It is also a reliable bloomer during the summer months. Lovely light pink tubular flowers bloom continuously in the hot season, and they attract hummingbirds during the day and sphinx moths at night. Give it morning sun or filtered shade. Mexican oregano can look a bit straggly during the cold months, so consider planting some annuals to fill in the holes; lobelia is appealing. No need to baby this plant in winter; it's hardy to the high teens. Prune it in late winter to encourage new growth.
- **Moss Verbena** (*Glandularia pulchella*) Low-growing but wide-spreading, moss verbena is ideal for spilling out of roomy containers, and its purple blooms attract nectar-hungry butterflies. Grow it in almost any orientation. Frost damage can occur in the mid-20s F, but plants recover quickly in spring.

FAR RIGHT: Mexican oregano (*Poliomintha maderensis*), is an olfactory delight.

RIGHT: Trailing lantana (*Lantana montevidensis*) trails nicely over the edges of containers.

BELOW: Shrimp plant (*Justicia brandegeana*).

- **Red Devil Verbena** (*Verbena peruviana* 'Red') Great for combining with taller perennials and succulents, red devil forms a low cover that will trail over the edge of containers.
- **Shrimp Plant** (*Justicia brandegeana,* syn. *Beloperone guttata*) Though this one needs some extra water, it performs well in containers and attracts hummingbirds. The flowers are white with purple spots and are enclosed in coppery-colored bracts that look like little shrimp. Give it morning sun in the summer. Pinch stems during the growing season to encourage bushiness.
- **'Starry Eyes' Nierembergia** (*Nierembergia gracilis* 'Starry Eyes') An Argentine desert native, 'Starry Eyes' is a good durable heat-tolerant plant for the low deserts. It has blue/lavender bell-shaped flowers and gets only 10 inches tall and 18 inches wide. Plant where it will receive at least six hours of sun each day.
- **Texas Betony** (*Stachys coccinea*) Texas betony might be the king spring bloomer of all hummingbird plants. This mint family plant produces copious red tubular flowers. Like other members of the family, it does best with regular water and appreciates some shade.
- **Trailing Lantana** (*Lantana montevidensis*) Lantanas are tough. This variety with purple flowers blossoms in late fall and early spring as well as during the summer months, and draws plenty of butterflies. It freezes easily but also recovers easily. Watch it tumble over the edges of a container.

- **'Ultra Violet' Sage** (*Salvia* 'Ultra Violet'), PPAF (awaiting patent approval) This cross between *S. lycioides* and *S. greggii* produces rose-purple flowers and is hardy to -15 degrees F.
- **'Valentine' Emu Bush** (*Eremophila maculata* 'Valentine'®) The perfect gift for Valentine's Day. This tough evergreen shrub begins blooming in late January and continues into February; it's not bothered by cold. Plant in full sun for optimal bloom. It draws hummingbirds and verdins. The latter pierce the bases of the flowers to obtain nectar. Give it a good haircut following bloom.
- **Velvet Honeysuckle** (*Dicliptera suberecta*) This native of Uruguay has soft-looking foliage and rusty orange tubular flowers that attract hummingbirds. Filtered shade is its preferred orientation in low desert areas. Although cold-hardy to about 15 degrees F, velvet honeysuckle may get leggy from winter temperatures. Prune in early spring to promote new growth.
- **'Violet Cloud' Skullcap** (*Scutellaria* 'Violet Cloud') A good low grower for filling in around other perennials. Grow skullcap as you would penstemons—providing good drainage and some supplemental watering during establishment.
- **Whirling Butterflies** (*Gaura lindheimeri* 'Pink Cloud') Whirling butterflies is tailor-made for a pot. Its graceful arching stems look like grass until it flowers with white- and pink-tinged blooms. The variety listed here, 'Pink Cloud,' produces hot-pink flowers. Whirling butterflies is hardy to -20 degrees F.

Perfumey Perennials

Sometimes it's the fragrance of a plant that attracts us the most. Brushing against aromatic foliage and stopping to smell the roses is one of the special pleasures of a day in the garden, and this is possible in container gardens as well. Try lavender (*Lavandula* spp.), hummingbird mint (*Agastache* 'Desert Sunrise'), Mexican oregano (*Poliomintha maderensis*), and chocolate flower (*Berlandiera lyrata*).

LEFT: A purple snapdragon vine (shown here) is small enough to be wedged in with many other succulents.

Tiny Native Vines for Pots

The following petite vines are particularly handsome when trained up small trellises (trellises can be as simple as sticking interesting tree branches into the potting soil). You can also use sculptural plants such as ocotillo or beaked yucca as "scaffolding" for these rambling vines.

TINY NATIVE VINES

PLANT NAME	MATURE HEIGHT	COLD HARDINESS (DEGREES F)	NOTES
Climbing Janusia (*Janusia gracilis*)	to 10', often smaller	18	Svelte little vine—nice on wire fencing.
Milkweed Vine (*Sarcostemma cynanchoides*)	to 15'	15	Available only from seed. Vastly underused.
Scarlet Creeper (*Ipomoea coccinea*)	to 10'	10	Little red fireworks on thin tendrils.
Snapdragon Vine (*Maurandya antirrhiniflora*)	to 10', often smaller	18	Delicate and tough. Great trained up an ocotillo.
Southwestern Pipevine (*Aristolochia watsonii*)	to 3'	15	Great for attracting pipevine swallowtail butterflies.

Bougainvilleas for Pots

Bougainvilleas are beloved plants in hot climates and lend a riot of color to the landscape. Small tubular blooms are surrounded by colorful, petal-like bracts that occur in clusters. Many of the species commonly sold get much too large and sprawly for containers. The following species are small selections that work well in pots:

- 'Rosenka' Bougainvillea (*Bougainvillea* 'Rosenka')
- 'Silhouette' Bougainvillea (*Bougainvillea* 'Silhouette')
- 'Torch Glow' Bougainvillea (*Bougainvillea* 'Torch Glow')

FAR RIGHT: A summer annual combo of cosmos, rose moss, and zinnias. Design: The Arizona Inn.

BELOW: Yellow marigolds are warm-season annuals.

Guaranteed Green

Although they are as common as old shoes, asparagus and foxtail ferns, *Asparagus densiflorus* 'Sprengeri' and *A. densiflorus* 'Myers' do remarkably well here. They require next-to-no attention, little water, and remain reliably green in sun or shade (foxtails prefer a bit more shade). Both thrive in containers, though eventually send out vigorous root systems that grow into the ground beneath. These are not plants that necessarily evoke a "sense of place," but they do provide refreshing, pleasing-to-the-eye green. Asparagus fern is ideal for cascading over the edge of a container.

ANNUAL COLOR: A NEW LOOK FOR EVERY SEASON

Temporary, seasonal color is a quick and easy way to liven up any landscape, and containers, large or small, provide the perfect venue. Seasonal color is most often provided

Defunct pickup trucks get a second life as planters filled with annuals.

by annuals—plants that germinate, grow, flower, set seed, and die over a period of several months. In general, annuals are fast growing and easy to grow. There are color choices galore—covering every hue of the rainbow—as well as a wide range of sizes, shapes, and bloom times. Massing plants of the same species is effective, but it is also possible to combine several different varieties to create a diverse display. Since annuals are less expensive than perennials, you can replace any plants that fail to thrive, or fail to suit your purposes, without breaking the bank. Give them well-drained soil rich in plant nutrients. Plantings of seasonal color are ideal for part-time residents who don't want a lot of muss and fuss. Even a small display can brighten a patio or entryway.

Although annuals can provide instant gratification, one of the ways they have been traditionally used in the Southwest—in wide swaths planted in the ground sometimes referred to as "carpet bedding"—is resource-intensive and probably unsustainable from a water-use perspective. Since arid soils are typically poor and often lacking in nutrients, growing annuals in the ground can require much coddling and irrigation. This is where containers seem like a much better alternative. You can provide splashes of higher-water-use color in very limited square footage, leaving the ground to more desert-adapted plants. In short, you can get your color fix without breaking the water bank, so to speak.

It is also possible to mix different annual combinations with perennials. Incorporate fall/winter-blooming annuals with summer-flowering perennials that have lost their appeal during the winter months; the annuals will mask the tired-looking leaves and/or bare stems of the potted perennial. Alyssum and lobelia make fine fillers for containers during the cool season. Annuals are also useful for filling in bare spots while other more permanent plantings take hold.

The choice of flower color or color combinations is largely a matter of personal taste, but regardless of size, a container will provide high visual impact when similar colors are grouped for a massed effect. Combining several distinct varieties with different flower colors can result in a haphazard look. In addition to color, using a wide array of textures and styles can make your containers more interesting.

Technically some plants, such as pansies, petunias, snapdragons, and stock, are classified as perennials or biennials, but they are better treated as annuals in our climate extremes. Perennial geraniums are often grown as cool-season annuals as well; these semi-succulent plants struggle through our hot summers, not blooming reliably at that time of year. Plant geraniums in containers in the fall for a colorful winter/spring show.

ABOVE: Group containers for greater aesthetic appeal.

BELOW LEFT: A colorful display with cosmos, yellow lantana, mealy cup sage, rose moss, and vinca.

Guilt-free Color

If you want bright colors in your garden without the hassle of annuals that have to be replaced twice each year, consider planting some cacti with colorful spines that will bring color to containers in a very low-maintenance package. The following are good choices that require little water:

- Arizona Rainbow Hedgehog Cactus (*Echinocereus rigidissimus*): red stripes
- Baja Fire Barrel (*Ferocactus gracilis* var. *coloratus*): red spines
- Fire Barrel (*Ferocactus pringlei*): red spines and ribs
- Golden Barrel (*Echinocactus grusonii*): golden yellow spines
- Golden Hedgehog (*Echinocereus nicholii*): golden yellow spines

Annual Wildflowers

To give your potted agaves, cacti, or euphorbias a few flashes of spring wildflower color, sow some native annual wildflower seeds. The best wildflower choices for succulent containers include Mexican gold poppies (*Eschscholzia mexicana*) and desert bluebells (*Phacelia campanularia*). These orange and gentian blue wildflowers are especially well suited to container culture and will live on the same watering regime as the sculptural plants. For best results, sow seeds into pots with gravel top dressings in fall while temperatures are still warm. Water lightly once a day until seedlings emerge, then just once per week until temperatures cool. If winter rains arrive, you will not have to water any more until spring. If the weather is dry, water the established seedlings twice per month from December through February.

At the Nursery

Search nurseries for new introductions, since choices vary year to year. Seed companies and wholesale growers currently use efficient and sophisticated techniques to speed up the production and evaluation of experimental plant hybrids and varieties. Their goal is to create larger, more intense or unusually colored flowers, and to grow plants with better heat and cold tolerance. So see what's available each season and experiment. Since seasonal-color plants come small (generally in four- or six-packs or in four-inch pots), they are less expensive than perennials and shrubs. This makes experimentation relatively inexpensive and enjoyable.

Select plants that are beginning to bud or flower so that you can be sure of bloom color, if that is important to you. Mislabeling is always a possibility. Look for plants with dark green leaves that are free of insect damage. Pale leaves may mean that the plant is running out of nitrogen and will get a slow start in your container, or possibly die off completely.

Most annuals grow readily from seed. If you start seasonal plants from seed it will save on the pocketbook, but it will also take a lot longer to achieve the desired effect. For immediate results, visit your local nursery and purchase already-established seedlings. Seed packets often provide a wider array of choices. However, be aware that some of the seeds offered in local garden centers and nurseries are not necessarily varieties that will succeed in the desert Southwest.

Take note that nursery tags often indicate that a plant requires "full sun" to thrive. This does not necessarily hold true for the arid Southwest, particularly during the summer months. Some of these "full sun" annuals will appreciate partial sun during the hottest months of the year.

Many nurseries offer pre-planted containers already filled to the brim with appropriate seasonal color. Generally, these color bowls are created by someone with skill in combining different sizes and shapes, colors, and textures. While these are tempting and can provide an immediate focal point in your outdoor space, they can be expensive. Also, sometimes these pre-planted containers are stuffed too tightly with plant material. Although this makes for a great impression initially, crowded plants may rapidly outgrow the container, forcing you to remove some or to watch the demise of others.

Seasonal Color through the Year

Annuals, or perennials/biennials that are treated as annuals, generally fall into two categories: 1) hardy, frost-resistant cool-season plants that bloom in late fall, winter, and

ABOVE: Eye-catching cabbage and kale: try combining a few herbs and a few seasonal flowers with ornamental cabbage or kale (grown specifically for their colorful foliage) for a pleasing display in the cool season.

BELOW RIGHT: Million bells (*Calibrachoa*), is related to the petunia. It's technically a perennial but is often grown as an annual.

early spring; and 2) frost-tender, heat-tolerant warm-season annuals that bloom in late spring, summer, and fall until killed by frost.

FALL/WINTER/EARLY SPRING BLOOMERS

- Calendula (*Calendula officinalis*)
- Cockscomb (*Celosia* spp.)
- Hollyhock (*Alcea rosea*)
- Iceland Poppy (*Papaver nudicaule*)
- Johnny-Jump-Up (*Viola tricolor*)
- Lobelia (*Lobelia erinus*)
- Nasturtium (*Tropaeolum majus*)
- Nicotiana (*Nicotiana alata*)
- Ornamental Cabbage and Kale (*Brassica* spp.)
- Pansy (*Pansy* x *wittrockiana*)
- Pentas (*Pentas lanceolata*)
- Petunia (*Petunia* hybrids)

For the Butterflies

Add motion and life to your container garden by planting cosmos (*Cosmos* spp.), coreopsis (*Coreopsis tinctoria*), Mexican sunflower (*Tithonia rotundifolia*), or zinnias (*Zinnia* spp.) By planting multiples of each species, you are more likely to catch the attention of passing butterflies.

- Phlox (*Phlox drummondii*)
- Shirley Poppy (*Papaver rhoeas*)
- Snapdragon (*Antirrhinum majus*)
- Stock (*Mathiola incana*)
- Sweet Alyssum (*Lobularia maritima*)
- Sweet Pea (*Lathyrus odoratus*)
- Sweet William (*Dianthus barbatus*)
- Viola (*Viola cornuta*)

SPRING/SUMMER/EARLY FALL BLOOMERS

- Coreopsis (*Coreopsis tinctoria*)
- Cosmos (*Cosmos bipinnatus, C. sulphureus*)
- Firewheel/Blanket Flower (*Gaillardia pulchella*)
- Globe Amaranth (*Gomphrena globosa*)
- Lisianthus (*Eustoma grandiflorum*)
- Marigold (*Tagetes erecta, T. patula*)
- Mexican Sunflower (*Tithonia rotundifolia*)
- Ornamental Pepper (*Capsicum annuum*)
- Rose Moss (*Portulaca* x hybrids)
- 'Victoria Blue' Sage (*Salvia farinacea* 'Victoria Blue')
- Vinca/Madagascar Periwinkle (*Catharanthus roseus*)
- Zinnia (*Zinnia angustifolia, Z. elegans*)

For the Birds

Tropical sage, *Salvia coccinea,* is a short-lived perennial but can be treated as an annual for best performance. Hummingbirds love the bright red tubular flowers, and goldfinches relish the seeds. The seed-grown selection 'Lady in Red' is not quite as popular with the birds.

Ornamental Peppers

Ornamental peppers (*Capsicum annuum*) are flashy little plants that are ideal for providing seasonal interest in container gardens. They come in many south-of-the-border hues, lending a true Southwestern feel to the landscape. Fruits may be round, curved, tapered, or thin, and colors change as they ripen from green/yellow to red/orange and even to purple in some varieties.

Watering and Fertilizing

After potting up your selections, it's important to remember that transplants often dry out quickly and may need daily watering until established, especially if the weather is hot or windy. As the plants begin to grow, water less often but apply more water each

Edible Flowers

Break up your culinary routine by adding some edible annuals to the mix. Johnny-jump-up (*Viola tricolor*), an old-time medicinal flower, can be added whole to salads or desserts. Brightly-colored flowers speak to the Southwest, and the large yellow, orange, or red blooms of nasturtium (*Tropaeolum majus*) taste peppery and enliven any salad. Sweet William (*Dianthus barbatus*) produces small ruffled blossoms in pastel color combinations that are clove-flavored; add to vegetable and fruit salads. Try freezing petals of these flower edibles in ice trays and enjoy some very festive ice cubes.

time to promote deep rooting. In general, annuals require fertile, well-drained soil that is kept evenly moist. Don't fertilize container-grown annuals until they have been planted for about two weeks. Once they show signs of active growth, begin fertilizing once every two weeks to maintain peak bloom. An organic mulch will help conserve soil moisture as well as keep down the weeds. Remove any weeds that crop up so they don't steal water or nutrients from the container's star attractions.

URBAN HERBS

Golden sage 'Aurea.'

Containers are ideal for growing aromatic herbs, which perform much better in potting soil than in nutrient-deficient, caliche-ridden desert soils. Many varieties come from Mediterranean or Middle Eastern regions and are often quite drought-tolerant.

Since many herbs are small in size, consider combining several kinds in large containers to produce more of an effect. But beware of using mints or oreganos, both of which have a tendency to take over, stealing space, water, and nutrients from other plants.

If you don't have room for large containers, or if weight is an issue, cluster smaller pots together for greater aesthetic appeal. By grouping them closely together, chores such as watering become easier as well. You can also place small pots on a raised rack or table so that they are more visible.

Care for Your Herbs

Use any good-quality, all-purpose potting soil for your herbs, and add some perlite or sand to ensure proper drainage. Soil mixes for herbs should not be mushy or peaty.

Reuse and recycle. Design: Tucson Botanical Gardens.

Herbs don't like wet feet so, as with other container plants, avoid using saucers. For summertime herbs, mulching the soil surface will help reduce evaporation.

Most herbs need sun. But during the hotter months, they appreciate sun in the morning and shade in the afternoon. Eastern exposures are ideal. You can move your herb pots into warmer exposures in late fall where they will enjoy the extra heat provided by the winter sun.

Potted herbs need to be watered adequately, and during the hot, dry months of summer, this might mean daily. As you water, try to keep the leaves dry, holding the hose at the soil level, and water until it comes out the bottom of the pot. Because of the frequency of watering needed to keep herbs happy during the hottest months, nutrients are leached out quickly, so fertilize once a month. If you plan to use herbs for cooking, you probably don't want to use synthetic fertilizers or pesticides. Fish emulsion works well and is completely safe. Water plants thoroughly before applying any liquid fertilizer.

Keep an eye on the weather. Once the monsoon season arrives, you can probably cut back on watering frequency. Some sage advice about the beloved herb lavender: It is particularly sensitive to increased humidity and has a tendency to rot if not allowed to dry out between waterings. Ditto for thyme.

Pinch your herbs often to encourage bushy growth and to enjoy the harvest. Never remove more than a third of the plant at any one time, so that growth is not compromised. It's a good idea to redo your herb pots about once a year, or to at least add some new, nutrient-filled soil. Fall is a good time.

That essential kitchen herb, rosemary, is not well suited for container gardening because its aggressive roots outgrow pots rapidly. If you decide to grow rosemary in a container, plant it by itself and replace it every year or two. Unlike rosemary, scented geraniums perform well when pot-bound, as do chives.

There are many varieties of scented geraniums: nutmeg, cinnamon, ginger, lemon, peppermint, and rose, to name a few. The leaves are the fragrant part of the plant and when brushed against release a delightful aroma. Scented geraniums don't like wet feet, so let them dry out between waterings. Pinch the branch tips to encourage new growth and to avoid that unwanted leggy look.

Plant herbs in containers close to the house so that watering chores may be accomplished more expediently and so that you can pop out and pinch a sprig here and there to add to whatever dish is on the menu.

Seasons for Herbs

Different kinds of herbs are suited to different seasons in the Southwest. Many are simply unable to take the heat of our summers and bolt easily. This means that the stems grow very rapidly and then flower in response to heat-induced stress. Annual herbs that fall into this category include dill, chervil, cilantro, chamomile, borage, caraway, and parsley. Try planting these in containers in the fall. Watch your parsley plants for the larvae of black swallowtails.

For you pesto fans, basil loves the summer heat but still prefers morning sun only. Basil plants will generally die off with the first frost of the season. Note that basil plants

For the Butterflies

Herbs in the parsley (Apiaceae) family serve as larval foodplants, fodder for the caterpillars of black swallowtail butterflies. Try these cool-season herbs (yes, we do indeed have butterflies on the wing year round in the desert Southwest):

- Dill (*Anethum graveolens*)
- Fennel (*Foeniculum vulgare*)
- Parsley (*Petroselinum graveolens*)

The caterpillars rarely do any permanent damage to plants, and by sharing the crop you are contributing to the creation of enchanting butterflies.

For the Hummingbirds

If you're an herb gardener, then lavender may already be part of your soul. Popular for centuries, lavender was regarded as an herb of love in the Middle Ages, and Romans added it to their bath water for the perfume. Grow lavender in containers for its sweet scent and lovely purple flower stalks that wave gently in the breeze. An added bonus is that the flowers attract hummingbirds. The rose-red flash of a male Anna's hummingbird in juxtaposition to the purple-blue flower spikes is dazzling. Tiny Costa's hummingbirds also visit the blossoms, drifting from flower to flower as they float in the breeze.

require large pots to perform well. Herbs such as oregano, thyme, and mint tend to be tough and can handle just about every season in the Southwest.

Heat-loving basil.

WARM-SEASON HERBS

- Basil (*Ocimum* spp.)
- Catnip (*Nepeta cataria*)
- Chives, Garlic Chives (*Allium* spp.)
- Epazote (*Dysphania ambrosioides*)
- Lavender (*Lavendula* spp.)
- Lemon Balm (*Melissa officinalis*)
- Mints (*Mentha* spp.)
- Oregano (*Origanum* spp.)
- Rosemary (*Rosmarinus officinalis*)
- Sages (*Salvia* spp.)
- Scented Geraniums (*Pelargonium* spp.)
- Thyme (*Thymus* spp.)

COOL-SEASON HERBS

- Chamomile (annual German: *Matricaria recutita*; perennial Roman: *Chamaemelum nobile*)
- Cilantro (*Coriandrum sativum*)
- Dill (*Anethum graveolens*)
- Garlic Chives (*Allium* spp.)

- Lavender (*Lavendula* spp.)
- Mints (*Mentha* spp.)
- Oregano (*Origanum* spp.)
- Parsley (*Petroselinum crispum*)
- Rosemary (*Rosmarinus officinalis*)
- Scented Geraniums (*Pelargonium* spp.)
- Thyme (*Thymus* spp.)

Annual, Perennial, and Biennial Herbs

Herbs may be annual, perennial, or biennial. Annual herbs germinate, grow, bloom, set seed, and die all in one season. Cilantro, dill, and chamomile are examples. Perennial herbs may go through dormant periods, but return year after year. Examples include lavender, thyme, oregano, sage, and mints. Biennial herbs germinate, grow, bloom, set seed, and die usually after two seasons. Parsley, borage, and caraway fit into this category.

It's Just about Thyme

There are different schools of thought about the origin of the genus name for thyme, an herb that partners well with dozens of foods. *Thymus* is Greek for "courage," a suitable designation for an herb that has an assertive quality. Others believe it is a derivation of a Greek term meaning "to fumigate." This, too, is appropriate for thyme, which was often burned in order to drive away nasty, biting insects. While you may be quite familiar with the commonly used English thyme (*Thymus vulgaris*), look for some more exotic choices to grow:

- Caraway Thyme (*T. herba-barona*)
- Conehead Thyme (*T. capitata—capitata* means "knob-like head.") One of our favorites (for the name if nothing else), conehead thyme is used in Mediterranean-style dishes.
- Creeping Thyme (*T. praecox* subsp. *arcticus*)
- Lemon Thyme (*Thymus* x *citriodorus*)

Lemony Herbs

No real lemons on hand? No worries; try using one of these luscious lemon-flavored herbs instead:

- Lemon Balm (Southern Europe, N. Africa): flavorings, tea, medicine
- Lemon Basil (Thailand): cooking

- Lemon Bergamot Mint (hybrid origin): tea, sachets
- Lemon Grass (Southeast Asia): cooking, tea, lemon grass oil
- Lemon-scented Geranium (South Africa): baking, sachets
- Lemon Thyme (Europe): teas, baking, sachets
- Lemon Verbena (South America): tea, sachets, medicine, cooking

Some Hot Herbs

- **Basils** (*Ocimum* spp.) are summer annuals that perform superbly in containers, although pots need to be on the large size in order to accommodate overly-enthusiastic roots. Try sweet basil, dark opal basil, or lemon basil for starters. These summer annuals grow quickly from seed or obtain starts from nurseries. Feed once a month with an organic fertilizer. Use sweet basil to make up batches of pesto throughout the growing season and freeze to enjoy year-round.
- **Cilantro** comes from the leaves of *Coriandrum sativum* (coriander is from the seeds). This cool-season annual is beloved in Mexican and Asian cooking, and loves the coziness of a container. The Chinese used coriander as far back as the Han dynasty, 207 B.C.–A.D. 220. Ingestion of the seeds was thought to make a person immortal.
- **Epazote** (*Dysphania ambrosioides*), also known as wormwood, is an annual herb that is valued in Mexican cooking. It's often used in dishes to offset the abdominal discomfort sometimes caused by beans but is also used in quesadillas and soups. Epazote grows well in containers in the warm season.

A MOVEABLE FEAST: VEGGIES IN CONTAINERS

Even in a challenging environment where sunlight is excessive, rainfall is sporadic, and daily temperatures can fluctuate by nearly 30 degrees F, one can successfully grow plenty of vegetables. And containers are the ideal solution if you don't have sufficient in-ground space.

Some people like to use raised beds (which essentially mimic large containers) for growing vegetables. By using stone, block, or water-resistant wood, you can create these beds for "containing" vegetable plants. Avoid chemically treated lumber or railway ties because their toxins can leach into your soil. Raised beds take time to build and can be expensive; in addition, they are immovable. Pre-made livestock water tanks, available at feed lot stores, are an excellent alternative, although some people don't care for their informal look. On a smaller scale, individual large pots work just fine for tomatoes, peppers, green onions, and some leafy greens.

Care for Your Veggies

Soil mixes for vegetable container plantings can be prepared and maintained much more easily than soil in the ground. A light soil mix won't require constant tilling; a light turn

Containers within this wooden box hold all the fixings for a winter salad.

with a hand trowel or cultivator may be all that is necessary. Containers filled with a light soil mix offer better drainage than in-ground gardens. By using large, pre-made containers such as livestock tanks (don't forget the drainage holes!), all of the soil space within is available for the plants—no need for pathways since plants are accessible from all sides. Since you won't need to walk among your veggies, soil compaction is less likely. Soil amendments and fertilizers are applied only to the areas where they are needed and are not wasted on pathways. The result: a higher yield in a smaller space. It's a good idea to revitalize your container garden soil mix once or twice a year with 4–6 inches of compost. Adding a mild fertilizer such as fish emulsion may also help.

Growing vegetables in containers may be more water-efficient than growing them in the ground. Since plants are close together, the soil is shaded, evaporation is decreased, and roots are more likely to stay cooler in the hot season. Beware, however, of overcrowding plants, which will result in poor air circulation as well as less exposure to necessary sunlight. Plant placement is important if you are combining different kinds of plants because shorter-growing varieties can be shaded out by taller ones. When plants are grown close together weeds are often deterred as well.

Most vegetables grow best in full sun, but there are exceptions. Full, all-day sun in June is pretty intense for any plant. Keep an eye out for plants that droop in the afternoon and/or show signs of sunburned leaves. Provide extra protection with shade cloth, available at garden centers and nurseries. Shade cloth blocks out some of the harsh rays of the sun but also enables air to continue to circulate to the plants.

In terms of day-to-day maintenance, vegetables grown in raised containers require less stooping and bending when it comes to tasks such as watering, weeding, and fertilizing, as well as harvesting. Taller containers (over 2 feet tall) may also help deter hungry critters such as rabbits, javelinas, or gophers.

A Veggie Growing Mix

Greg Corman of Gardening Insights in Tucson, Arizona, recommends the following mix for growing vegetables in containers: one part pumice, one part sand, one part loam soil, and three parts composted organic matter. He also favors amending garden soil with rock phosphate, mineral sulfur, and an organic form of nitrogen such as composted manure or kitchen waste.

Seasons for Veggies

There are essentially two growing seasons for vegetables here: the cool season (October to April) and the warm season (April to October). Cool-season plants enjoy shorter days and lower temperatures. Warm-season vegetables prefer heat and long hours of sunshine. Cool-season vegetable gardens are generally more productive. The growing season can be expanded since raised containers warm up faster and crops can be planted earlier. Short-season crops such as radishes, lettuce, and other salad greens mature quickly enough that a second batch can be planted mid-winter after the first crop is harvested.

COOL-SEASON CROPS

- Arugula
- Asian Broccoli
- Asian Greens
- Beets
- Bok Choi
- Broccoli
- Broccoli Raab
- Brussels Sprouts
- Cabbage
- Carrot
- Cauliflower
- Chinese Cabbage
- Collard Greens
- Garlic
- Kale
- Kohlrabi
- Leek
- Lettuce
- Mustard Greens
- Onion
- Peas
- Radish
- Spinach
- Swiss Chard
- Turnips

WARM-SEASON CROPS

- Amaranth
- Beans
- Chiles
- Corn
- Cucumber
- Eggplant
- Okra
- Peppers
- Summer Squash
- Tomato

A Note about Tomatoes

Unlike in other regions of North America, tomatoes should be planted in most areas here as early as February; that, of course, is assuming that you can protect them from frost. Tomatoes need time to flower, produce fruits, and ripen before the onslaught of the brutal heat of summer. Short-season varieties work well. Shade cloth for sun protection is another possibility if you get them in too late.

Sprawling Edibles

You can attempt to grow sprawling plants such as melons or gourds in containers, but they take up a lot of space. Try rigging up some sort of trellis or cage so that these floppy plants don't take over.

Don't forget the cherry tomatoes.

Chile Roastin'

It's difficult to imagine Southwestern cooking without chile peppers. Here's a quick way to roast a chile. Fire up a gas stove burner, grab a long green chile with a pair of tongs (wooden handles preferred) and turn it slowly in the flame until it blisters and the kitchen begins to smell good. If the pepper is too dry, it may catch fire, so beware. Place peppers in a bag and allow them to sweat for 15 minutes; this will make them easier to peel. Rinse under cool running water (wear gloves to avoid contact with skin), peel, remove, and discard skin and seeds. Toss these quick-roasted chiles into a Crock-Pot with a batch of beans or into soup, or use with the chicken you're sautéing for dinner.

'Thai Dragon' peppers.

Seeds and Transplants

You can start vegetables either from seeds or transplants from nurseries. Seeds offer the greatest choices and are less expensive than buying nursery seedlings. If you use seeds, start four to eight weeks prior to transplanting into the garden. Seedlings are ready to transplant when they are about 3–4 inches tall.

Citrus

Citrus plants enjoy our Southwestern heat but don't like freezing temperatures. Nonetheless, it's possible to grow dwarf varieties in large containers, particularly if you live in a warm belt, or if you are willing to make the effort to protect plants from the cold. Citrus plants do require ample water for successful fruits, but the rewards are great: tasty limes for those gin and tonics, zingy kumquats for marmalade, sweet Meyer lemons for cooking—the list goes on. Plants are evergreen and have fragrant blossoms. Another plus: the caterpillars of showy giant swallowtail butterflies eat the leaves of cultivated citrus; the caterpillars resemble bird droppings, a form of disguise against predators.

Dwarf citrus are budded on an understock of trifoliate orange (*Poncirus trifoliata*) called 'Flying Dragon.' 'Flying Dragon' rootstock controls the ultimate size of plants. Check with your nursery person to be sure you are purchasing a dwarf variety; reliable nurseries can readily identify the rootstock on which a plant was grafted.

Doing the Wild Pepper

Wild chiltepin (*Capsicum annuum* v. *aviculare*) grows well in containers and has culinary, ornamental, and wildlife value. Fiery hot chiltepines are the crowning touch for many spicy dishes. Vividly red fruits ripen quickly and stand erect on the stems, sticking out above the foliage where they are obviously visible for passing birds. This plant is so associated with birds that many of its common names suggest the relationship: bird pepper, *pajaro pequeño* (little bird), and *pico pajaro* (bird's beak). Birds, unlike other creatures such as humans or mammals, are not bothered by the fiendish heat of this wild pepper. In particular, mockingbirds and thrashers enjoy the nutritious fruits, and tiny verdins seem to relish them as well.

H_2O

The veggie garden is no place to skimp on water; remember that you are trying to grow food, not merely attempting to keep a plant alive! During the hot dry months plants may require watering as frequently as twice a day (depending on size of container); by

Native Seeds/SEARCH

Native Seeds/SEARCH, a Tucson-based organization, is dedicated to conserving agricultural seeds of a diverse variety of plants that have played a role in the cultures of the American Southwest and Northwestern Mexico. Shop their online catalog for such edible delights as Tepehuan tomatillo, Mrs. Burns' Famous Lemon Basil, Texas Wild Tomato, I'itoi's onion, and O'odham green peas. (See "Hot Pot Resources" on page 120 for contact info.)

Stock tank planters, shown here at Tohono Chul Park, are excellent as veggie containers, but remember to make drainage holes.

contrast, others may require watering only two times per week in winter. Keeping soil moist but not soggy is best for vegetables. Veggies should not be allowed to dry out completely. Stick your finger down about ½ inch into the soil to see if it's still moist. If it's dry, then it means it's time to water. Underwatering can lead to poor fruit production or even the demise of a plant, while overwatering can cause root rot and stunted growth.

It's a good idea to avoid overhead watering which may damage seedlings or young plants. Overhead watering during the heat of summer can result in leaf burn. Mulching your containers will help keep the soil from drying out too quickly. Fertilizing may increase fruit production, but adding organic matter on a regular basis can eliminate the need for fertilizing. Drip irrigation lines can certainly be installed in vegetable container gardens. If you are using standard drip emitters, you will need to experiment to see how many emitters you need to saturate the root zone of your potted veggies. Drip emitters are available with flow rates from ½ gallon per hour to 5 gallons per hour. Soaker hoses, with perforations that let water seep into the ground, are another possibility for stock tanks or humongous containers. If you are watering by hand during the warm season, remember to run the water in the hose for a minute or two before applying to plants. Hoses heat up very quickly and you don't want to apply scalding water to your plants.

CHAPTER 4:

Soils

THE DIRT ON DIRT

Plants may get all the *oohs* and *aahs*, but good-looking plants begin with a healthy planting medium. Healthy soils contain organisms that improve water and air exchange and break down organic matter into nutrients required for plant growth.

The potting mix used for growing plants in containers is of utmost importance. Regular garden soil is too dense to use. A good potting mix will contain air, an element that is necessary for plant roots to fulfill their function; that is, the uptake of water and the growing of more roots. Without sufficient air, roots may decline and plants may weaken or die. Regular garden soil, in addition to being too dense, is also lacking in organic material and may contain grubs or other creatures that are harmful to plants. Plants that are grown in containers need a mix that drains well, is absorbent, lightweight, and free of pests and diseases.

Thankfully, a myriad of commercial potting mixes is now available at nurseries and garden centers, and even at some grocery stores. Pre-mixed soils are generally sterilized so that they are disease- and weed-free. They are usually sold in cubic-foot bags. Although the smaller-sized bags (less than one cubic foot) are lightweight and useful if you're planting on a limited scale, they are not particularly economical. Larger-sized bags are a better deal, if you can manage them. As a general rule, a one-cubic-foot bag will fill approximately two 12-inch-wide pots.

Although often labeled "potting soil," pre-packaged mixes rarely contain any real soil. They are composed of any number of materials including sphagnum peat moss, compost, forest products, perlite, pumice, vermiculite, charcoal, sand, and occasionally water-holding polymers.

Superabsorbent polymers are gels that absorb hundreds of times their weight in water. When mixed into potting soil, they hold water extremely well, swelling to many times their normal size. Polymers release water slowly into the root zone and are rehydrated each time the plant is watered. Their presence can increase the number of days between waterings, a useful feature in hot, dry climates.

When looking at all-purpose mixes at the nursery, check the labels to determine the ingredients. As with anything else, there are choices. Combinations vary, and a few mixes contain controlled-release fertilizers, an added component that appeals to many.

Some gardeners prefer to use specialty mixes, also widely available, for different kinds of plantings. There are cactus mixes which sometimes contain pumice, earthworm castings, compost, and forest humus. Mixes for seedling starts may include peat moss,

Having some basic supplies on hand makes impromptu planting easy.

perlite, and some sort of wetting agent. "Waterhold" blends may contain coconut fibers, peat moss, earthworm castings, and pumice. Mixes claiming to be natural and organic may be comprised of earthworm castings, peat, compost, forest humus, perlite, and pumice. If you wish to be sure that your potting soil is organic, buy bags that are certified by OMRI (Organic Materials Review Institute). This might be particularly important for container-grown edible plants such as veggies and herbs.

COMMON POTTING MIX INGREDIENTS

Ground-up or Shredded Forest Products

These products have a woody, coarse texture. Too much of this in coarser (and often less expensive) mixes results in diminished water-holding capacity. In addition, as woody components decompose, they rob plants of nutrients—not the other way around. This component, in the right proportion, however, lends structure to a mix. Composted forest mulch is more aged than some of the shredded products and is a good soil conditioner, immediately supplying nitrogen to plants.

Compost

Compost may contain small amounts of shredded wood but is composed largely of vegetative material. It is generally well broken down, contains a lot of nutrients, and is excellent for vegetables, roses, and perennials.

Peat

Peat is partially decomposed, ancient plant material such as mosses and sedges that are mined from boggy areas. Peat holds water and is slightly acidic. In the right proportion (about one-third) it is a nice addition to any mix. Since it holds water like a sponge, it needs to be thoroughly mixed with the other soil mix ingredients; it is difficult to rewet once it dries out. Mixes with too much peat can turn into tight blocks in containers, causing water to run down the sides of the root ball rather than penetrating it. Some people feel it is not environmentally responsible to use peat moss because peat bogs do not renew themselves.

Pumice, Perlite, and Vermiculite

Pumice and perlite are extremely lightweight volcanic substances that may be added to mixes to prevent soil compaction. They hold air in the root zone but provide no nutrients.

Vermiculite is mica that has been heated and looks like little worms made up of many layers. These layers allow it to absorb and hold water and air.

These minerals do not directly provide nutrients, but they are elements for good drainage. In containers where a portion of the soil surface is visible, you may wish to avoid soils with perlite because the little white beads tend to float up to the soil surface when the pot is heavily watered, creating an unsightly layer. Even when the soil is top-dressed with gravel, perlite can work its way to the surface. For this reason, mixes with pumice or vermiculite are generally a better choice because they are both darker and don't float as easily.

CONCOCTING YOUR OWN MIX

If you'd like to experiment and try something different than what's commercially available, think about concocting your own mix. You've probably heard some gardeners referring to "secret mixes" which cause their annuals to pop and their roses to flourish. The thing to remember here is that different soil textures influence the movement of water.

One way to begin making your own mix is to dump some potting soil into a wheelbarrow and then doctor it up. When planting cacti, for example, you might use 50% high quality potting soil and 50% pumice or perlite, plus a little sand to improve drainage. For roses, you might stretch your potting soil with 25% homemade sifted compost. For herbs, some people like to use 25% pumice or perlite mixed with a commercial blend. For vegetables, stir in some compost and a handful of composted steer manure. Note, however, that steer manure is salty by nature and too much of it can cre-

Common Ingredients at a Glance

Ground bark: doesn't hold water or nutrients but is less expensive than peat
Compost: holds water and nutrients, and drains
Peat moss: acidic, holds water but is salty
Pumice: helps with drainage, lacks nutrients
Perlite: helps with drainage, lacks nutrients
Vermiculite: helps with drainage, lacks nutrients but holds them
Sand: heavy, but drains and supports

ate a problem with salt buildup. Also be aware that there are some materials which should not be used in potting soil blends—notably ashes, sawdust, and non-composted manures. A couple of large plastic garbage cans with lids work well for storing your homemade mix.

Once you have your potting mix and an appropriately sized container in hand, you're ready to plant. Gently break up the root ball, place the plant in the container and fill with potting mix. But don't fill the container completely to the top; otherwise you run the risk of spilling out the mix every time you water.

Decomposed granite is a good top dressing for succulents.

SOIL MIXES FROM THE EXPERTS

Plants for the Southwest Cacti/Succulent Mix

Jane Evans and Gene Joseph, owners of Plants for the Southwest in Tucson, Arizona, recommend the following planting mix: 50% pumice, 20% peat moss, 20% mulch (decomposed fir bark), 5% sand, 5% vermiculite. Jane and Gene also add the lowest recommended application rate of slow release fertilizer (such as Osmocote) to their mix.

Russ Buhrow's Native Plant and Cacti/Succulent Mix

Russ Buhrow is the Curator of Plants at Tohono Chul Park in Tucson and his simple mix is excellent for a variety of native perennials and cacti/succulents that require very fast draining soil. He uses 50% mortar sand and 50% ¼-minus (particles small enough to fit through a screen with ¼-inch holes) screened compost.

Greg Starr's Agave and Native Plant Mix

Tucson plantsman and agave expert Greg Starr uses this mix for all his desert plants: 60% pumice, 20% sharp sand (also called masonry sand), and 20% ¼ inch minus (particles small enough to fit through a screen with ¼-inch holes) compost. For leafy plants (perennials and annuals), Starr adds 5-10-10 fertilizer.

THE LIFE OF A SOIL MIX

Clearly in an environment as harsh as the desert Southwest, soil mixes don't last forever. With the amount of watering necessary to sustain life, nutrients are continually being washed out of container-grown plants. As soils dry up, salts evaporate and collect on the insides and outsides of pots.

If you are re-potting seasonally, it's fine to discard the mix along with the plants. But potting mixes can get expensive. It's absolutely okay to re-use the soil mix from an old container, but only if the plants formerly occupying it did not suffer from any kind of blight or disease. As a middle ground, try mixing some new potting soil in with the old,

Weathered, peeling pots have their own charm.

and perhaps consider adding some drain-enhancing material. However, think about what you are planting. You wouldn't want to plant a cactus in an old soil mix that you previously used for vegetables. Also note that over time, the bulkier organic elements of potting mixes break down into humus, organic matter derived from partially decomposed plant remains. This causes the mix to become more dense, at which point it loses its structure, and roots may completely fill the container. For these reasons, we eventually need to repot long-lived plants in order to keep them healthy.

FAR LEFT: Pots "planted" in the ground overflow with hardy ice plant (*Delosperma cooperi*). Design: Denver Botanic Garden.

CHAPTER 5:

Care and Feeding

ONCE YOU'VE PLANTED YOUR CONTAINERS, they will, of course, require attention: weeding, fertilizing, and, the most critical factor of all, watering. Too much or too little H_2O is probably the main reason plants fail. If you neglect to water frequently enough, leaves can turn yellow, develop scorched edges, or in severe cases, become so stressed that they drop off the plant. On the other hand, too much water can result in root rot and the demise of a plant. Judging how much water to apply is relatively easy. If you are watering by hand, always apply water until it runs out the drainage hole at the bottom of the container.* This prevents salt buildup, and excess salts make for poor plant growth. But how often to water is another story.

* The only exception to this rule is when you are watering winter-growing succulent plants from South Africa, such as aloes, in the hottest part of summer. During the hot and humid summer months, these plants prefer to be lightly watered, or sprinkled, rather than soaked. See "Aloe Watering: Getting Your African Plants through the Summer" (page 47).

WATERING FREQUENCY

RIGHT: Mexican gold poppies—grown by seed—are great companions to agaves such as Queen Victoria.

FAR RIGHT: Bringing a potted plant like this grizzly bear prickly pear into a garden bed makes it a focal point.

Frequency is based on a number of variables: the type of plant; its stage of growth; type of container; size of container; potting mix; use of mulch or top dressings; orientation; and weather conditions.

Type of Plant

While veggies and annuals like to be moist, cacti and succulents insist on dry conditions. Semi-succulents such as geraniums require more water than cacti and succulents, but probably less than other perennials. Depending on their level of drought tolerance, most perennials probably fall somewhere in between. Know the water requirements of your plants.

Stage of Growth

Frequency of watering depends in part on the stage of growth of a plant. Newly planted material may need watering daily. Mature, established plants, on the other hand, may require less. Plants with lots of top growth in relation to the size of the pot, or plants with large leaves that transpire water rapidly, may need to be watered as often as twice a day in the hot season.

Type of Container

The type of pot you select will affect watering schedules. Porous containers, such as terra-cotta, give plant roots plenty of oxygen and don't stay soggy since the container

actually absorbs excess moisture; they can dry out quickly and will need to be watered more often. On the other hand, nonporous pots, such as plastic, do not allow for the free passage of air and moisture, so potting mixes remain wet longer; avoid overwatering. Some containers, such as glazed or dark-colored pots, heat up more quickly if placed in full sun. See further discussion of porous vs. non-porous containers in Chapter 1, "Selecting Pots" (pages 15–34).

Size of Container

First, do some homework in terms of plant growth rates and size so that you can select an appropriately sized container. Obviously, larger pots hold water longer than tiny pots. Tiny pots can be a nightmare in the summer unless planted with cacti or succulents.

Arranging striking potted specimens along the edge of a patio gets them noticed.

Potting Mix

How quickly a potting mix holds water and how quickly it drains are important variables in terms of watering frequency. See further discussion in "The Dirt on Dirt" (page 93).

Use of Mulches or Top Dressings

Applying a layer of mulch to your containers, or using top dressings, helps hold in moisture by decreasing evaporation and keeping roots cool.

Orientation

If a pot sits in full sun all day long in the summer months, it will probably require more water than a container placed in part or full shade. Reflected heat also plays a role here. Walls, patios, and pavement can all absorb heat on sunny days; the heat radiates outward and nearby plants can take a beating.

Weather Conditions

The hot, dry months of May and June (when a missed day of watering can spell death for a plant) are quite different from July, August, and early September when monsoonal moisture often enters the scene. Increased humidity and rainfall requires us to adjust our watering schedules in order to avoid rotting out some plants. Overwatering can also be a problem on cloudy days or in cool weather. Wind dries out plants very quickly, particularly those in containers, so watering may need to be stepped up during windy weather.

A FEW WATERING TIPS

Place a flowhead, or water breaker, on your hose to break the force of water; otherwise, you might displace soil. Watering wands (aluminum tubes capped with sprinkler heads) break the force of water and are available at most garden centers and nurseries. Many watering wands also have on/off levers so that you can turn off the water as you move from one location to the next; it pays to be water-thrifty here.

Remember that unrelenting sunshine can heat up hoses that are sitting out in the open. Before applying hose water to plants, let water run for a few moments until it cools off in order to avoid burning plants.

Apply water to the potting mix and not to the leaves of the plant. Water on leaves can cause scorching or burning in bright sunlight. Fully saturate the potting soil when you water, and apply water until it comes out the drainage hole. This will prevent salt buildups, a result of lots of watering as well as the use of fertilizers. Saucer watering (letting the container sit in a wet saucer to draw up water) also increases the possibility of salt buildup.

USING DRIP

If you don't have time for hand watering or are going to be gone a lot, consider hooking up your pots to a drip irrigation system. This offers convenience and enables you to actually leave town every once in a while! Through tubes and emitters, water is delivered directly to the root zones of your plants, and little is lost to runoff or evaporation. Drip irrigation systems may be operated manually or placed on automated timers. Since black poly tubing can be a bit unsightly when fed over the rim of a pot, think about inserting the tubing up through the drainage hole of the container for a more aesthetic appearance. Just remember that the latter may be more difficult to replace as plant roots grow and surround the tubing.

The most important thing to remember when setting up a drip system for potted plants is to set up an irrigation zone (also called a valve) specifically for the pots that is separate from your in-ground plants; container specimens need more frequent watering, particularly during the summer months. To work best, run the system for several hours to completely saturate the soil. An option for large containers is to attach an emitter with multi-outlets to the poly tubing. The multi-outlet bubbler sends water out in all directions.

If you decide to use drip irrigation, it is important to give your containers a deep soak with the hose periodically in order to flush out salt buildup. Saturate the soil and water thoroughly until water comes out the bottom of the container.

Deep-water Ollas

The use of deep-water ollas is an ancient Native American watering technique with a long history of use in the Southwest. Fill these handmade, unglazed, porous jars with water and bury them neck-deep in the soil surrounding your plants. Water gently seeps into the soil and is absorbed by plant roots. A source for deep-water ollas is High Country Gardens in Santa Fe, New Mexico: www.highcountrygardens.com, (800) 925-9387.

FERTILIZING

Just as there are potting mixes to choose from, there are fertilizer choices as well. Both synthetic and organic fertilizers come in various forms: granular or powdered; soluble crystals or emulsions; and pelleted (slow release).

Chemical fertilizers are made from petroleum and mined materials. They are synthesized and extensively processed and generally come in all three forms noted above. Chemical fertilizers work quickly to deliver nutrients but do not last long. Organic fertilizers are made from materials derived from plants and animals, as well as from minimally processed minerals. They are usually in granular/powdered or emulsion form. Organics are slower acting but last longer. Use organics on the plants you plan to eat.

The three nutrients typically listed on fertilizer analysis labels are N, P, and K. These are the chemical abbreviations for nitrogen (N), phosphorus (P), and potassium (K), the primary nutrients required for plant growth. Nitrogen promotes leaf and stem growth; phosphorus promotes strong roots as well as the formation of flowers, fruits and seeds; and potassium supports overall plant growth.

Granular or Powdered

Granular or powdered fertilizers, the most economical, need to dissolve into the soil and then get broken down by microorganisms. Synthetic varieties may cause damage to some plants if they come in direct contact with the roots since they draw water out of the root cellular structure. Powdered organics such as blood, bone, or fish meal provide nutrients slowly, so they are probably a better choice for perennials rather than annuals.

Soluble Crystals

Soluble crystals, when dissolved in water, are almost immediately available to plants. They may keep your plants looking good but may need to be applied more often. Emulsions such as fish and seaweed preparations take longer because they need soil microorganisms to break them down. Organic emulsions often smell bad until they break down, and pets may be attracted to the odor. You can't beat the convenience of soluble crystals and emulsions because they are applied during watering.

Pelleted

Pelleted types of fertilizer are convenient because they require infrequent applications; however, they are the most expensive. The pelleted forms need water or heat over a period of time in order to release the nutrients contained within. Pelleted forms always work better when mixed with the soil. Stick them in the potting mix when first setting plants; then replenish every three months or so by scratching them into the surface of the potting mix.

For most plants, a pelleted form of fertilizer might last several months. Slow-release water-soluble varieties, on the other hand, need to be applied much more frequently—every two weeks during the growing season. Some container gardeners recommend using a combination of the two.

Iron deficiencies are common in container-grown plants in the Southwest. Iron is immobilized by excessive levels of phosphate and other salts or chemical bases, resulting in a severe loss of chlorophyll. The most obvious symptom of iron deficiency chlorosis is usually the yellowing of the leaf area between the veins. This is best treated with slow-release chelated iron.

The outsides of terra-cotta pots often develop a crusty white coating from dissolved fertilizers (especially chemical fertilizers) and/or salt buildups. The coating is left as water evaporates from the outside of a pot. This is generally not a problem for the plants, but if you find it unsightly it can be removed. Water the coated container well. After the pot absorbs some of the water and seems moist, use a brush to scour off the deposits. If deposits return quickly, this may indicate that you are using too much fertilizer.

ROOT BOUND!

A container is a self-contained unit and the potted plant's space is somewhat restricted as a result. When you notice roots growing through the drainage hole and/or your plant is looking stressed, it may be time to shift up to a larger container. Shallow-rooted, seasonal annuals typically do not have problems in this regard, but larger perennials, shrubs, and trees will fail to thrive if their roots become too crowded. The larger the plant, the more extensive is its root system.

These plants may outgrow the container in short order.

UP POTTING

There are various other terms for this, including "potting on" and "potting up." Technically speaking, "potting on" means transplanting a plant into the next-sized container, while "potting up" refers to transplanting seedlings or cuttings from a flat into individual containers. Whatever you want to call it, plants that are root bound will appreciate being relocated into a container that gives them more space for their roots to grow.

When selecting a larger container for transplanting plant material, think about its size. You want to shift up to a container that is only slightly larger. Generally you want to use a pot that is one or two sizes larger (approximately two inches in diameter bigger). Your plant won't look right if you move it into a container that is much too large.

Be sure the new container has adequate drainage holes, and place a small piece of screening or a pottery shard over the drainage hole to prevent soil loss.

Fill the new container partially with soil mix. Consider adding a time-release fertilizer. Gently remove the plant from the smaller pot by turning the plant and its root ball upside down. Separate and untangle roots on the outside of root ball with your hands, or if the root ball is very compacted, use a sharp knife to cut down its sides; this will encourage the roots to move out into new soil. Add potting mix to the bottom and sides of the container, placing the top of the root ball one to two inches below the container rim. The plant should be planted no deeper than it was in its old container. Add more potting mix around the root ball, pressing firmly to eliminate air pockets. New potting mix combined with a slow-release fertilizer will give the plant a fresh start in its new home. Add a layer of mulch if you so desire and then water thoroughly.

A Note on Shape

If you select rounded containers that lack tapering sides, you will discover transplanting to be an extremely difficult task. Adding and replacing soil will be challenging as well. Sometimes a rounded pot must be broken in order to remove the plant. The tapering sides of most containers make it relatively easy to slide out plants for potting up.

ABOVE: This ball glows in the dark.

FAR LEFT: Foxtail fern with embellishments.

CHAPTER 6:

Finishing Touches

TOP DRESSING AND MULCH FOR POTS

Once your pots are planted, you will probably want to cover up the unplanted soil surface with some sort of mulch or top dressing. Mulch not only improves the appearance of the pot, it also conserves water by reducing evaporation and suppresses weed growth. Top dressing comes in two basic varieties: organic (shredded bark, compost, etc.), or inorganic (gravel and rock). Organic mulch is best for most herbaceous perennials and annuals, while inorganic mulches are excellent for sculptural plants. For mulches to be effective in suppressing weeds and reducing soil evaporation, they should be spread between two and three inches thick.

Organic Mulches

BARK MULCH Probably the most common organic top dressing, bark mulch comes either shredded or in chunks. For most containers, shredded is best (bark chunks tend to float away). A bark mulch that has been composted is best.

Chunky riprap mulch is a bold top dressing for this fire barrel cactus.

Compost

Compost is one of the best soil-building amendments and it is also a great product for retaining surface soil moisture. Because it will decompose and blend into the soil, it will feed your plants as well; for this reason, you'll need to reapply it every few months to maintain a sufficient layer.

Composted Pecan Hulls

These handsome dark brown and black hulls make excellent top dressing. Like compost, they decompose (albeit more slowly) and will need to be topped off from time to time.

Inorganic Mulches

For cacti, agaves, yuccas, and other sculptural plants, adding geology (in the form of a gravel mulch) is both good for reducing evaporation and handsome to boot. Since many succulent plants grow in rocky conditions, mimicking natural habitat in pots makes good sense. The following three products work well with sculptural plants. Rock products can be purchased at sand and gravel supply companies. Glass products are available online (see "Hot Pot Resources" on page 121).

GRAVEL Gravel, also known as "decorative rock," comes in a variety of sizes such as ⅜-, ½-, ⅝-, ¾-, and 1-inch pieces. It also comes in a rainbow of colors from light tan to rose red. Gravel is typically a "screened rock" product, meaning that if you order ¼-inch gravel you get a smaller portion (typically 30–40 percent) of rocks smaller than ⅜ of an inch, which are also known as fines (powdery dirt-like crushed-rock material).

RIPRAP Riprap is larger, angular, and chunky rock material. Like gravel, it comes in a variety of colors. Its sizes range from 1–3-inch pieces to 4–8-inch pieces. It works particularly well in large pots where big specimens are planted (think ocotillos). Wildflowers seed well in riprap.

GLASS MULCH For containers planted with long-lived sculptural plants that can be left in the same pot for several years before up-potting, a sparkling glass mulch might be considered. This is particularly effective in pots with planted with columnar cactus such as snow pole or Mexican fencepost where the footprint of the plant leaves a lot of visible potting soil. Glass mulch is also well-matched to clean-lined modern pots. It comes in a rainbow of colors: from semi-transparent glacier greens which evoke the look of ice, to dark cobalt blues, ambers, emeralds, and mixes. It is typically available in three sizes: small (¼- to ½-inch-diameter pieces); medium (½- to 1-inch-diameter pieces); and large (1- to 2-inch-diameter pieces). Larger glass pieces, sometimes called "glass rocks," are

Add color with recycled bottles.

between 2 and 6 inches in diameter and resemble glass riprap. Glass rocks can have sharp edges, so they should be kept out of pots that might be accessible to children and pets. Glass is not a good choice for pots planted with annuals or other plants that require frequent cultivation or replacement, as the glass is relatively expensive and hard to keep separated from potting soil.

ACCESSORIZING TO PERK UP YOUR POTS

Surrounding ourselves with living plants makes us feel better in many ways, including appealing to our aesthetic senses. Sometimes, however, our creative urges kick into high gear, and we find ourselves wanting to further embellish our living works of art. Combining plants with various inert objects has become quite the rage. Inanimate objects may be simple, elegant, or whimsical—whatever appeals to your individual taste.

Simply adding some attractive rocks can add to a container's appeal. Plant stakes come short or tall and are made of various materials. Plop one in a pot to create an artistic touch. Nature lovers might enjoy those rusted stakes topped with flowers, butterflies, or dragonflies. If you enjoy spending time out of doors at dusk, there are plant stakes with glow-in-the-dark balls at the top.

More dramatic statements may be made with sculptures of various kinds. There's something for everyone: people, birds, cats, frogs, turtles, lizards, rabbits, and the list goes on. Sculptures are particularly useful during seasons when container perennials are not at their best, diverting the eye away from the non-thriving plants. Check your local nursery or garden center for the latest in garden art to perk up your pots.

Craft-oriented folks might contemplate decorating their terra-cotta containers with paint. You should clean the container well (or use a brand new pot). Seal inside and out with a terra-cotta sealer. Let dry for at least 24 hours. Brush latex paint on the outside of the container to create a base color; let dry thoroughly and then apply a second coat. Then use stencils, brushes, sponges, or spatter paint to decorate. Or create your own freehand designs with stripes, dots, triangles, flowers, or leaves—whatever strikes your fancy.

LABELING YOUR PLANTS

If you find yourself getting more and more plants and getting slightly confused as to what's what, you may wish to use labels. These come in various styles and shapes. There are tie-ons, as well as swinging or flag styles. You can choose small, functional types or those that are larger, more whimsical and decorative. In terms of marking products, pencil works reasonably well in terms of standing up to the elements, but an even better choice is an opaque paint marker. (DecoColor is one brand that is reliable, weatherproof, and permanent.) These pens provide truly permanent markings and don't fade even in the unrelenting sunshine of the Southwest. They also resist water.

Add a decorative metal stake to liven up a container. Birds like to perch on them, too.

Use labels to help keep track of what you plant.

HOT POT RESOURCES

Arizona

Arid Lands Greenhouses
3560 West Bilby Road
Tucson, AZ 85746
520-883-9404

Arizona-Sonora Desert Museum
2021 N Kinney Rd
Tucson, AZ 85743
520-883-2702, www.desertmuseum.org

B & B Cactus Farm
11550 East Speedway Boulevard
Tucson, AZ 85748
520-721-4687, www.bandbcactus.com

Bach's Cactus Nursery
8602 North Thornydale Road
Tucson, AZ 85742
520-744-3333, www.bachs-cacti.com

Civano Nursery
5301 South Houghton Road
Tucson, AZ 85747
520-546-9200, www.civanonursery.net

Desert Survivors Native Plant Nursery
1020 West Starr Pass Boulevard
Tucson, AZ 85713
520-361-3071

Gardening Insights (landscape design)
1800 North Norton Avenue
Tucson, AZ 85719
520-603-2703, www.gardeninginsights.com

The Green Goddess
4139 East Bell Road
Phoenix, AZ 85032
800-428-4612, www.greengoddess.com

Harlow Gardens
5620 East Pima Street
Tucson, AZ 85712
520-298-3303, www.harlowgardens.com

Kornegay Design (cast concrete planters)
212 South 18th Street
Phoenix, AZ 85034
877-252-6323, www.kornegaydesign.com

Landscape Cacti
7711 West Bopp Road
Tucson, AZ 85735
520-883-0020

La Paloma de Tubac
1 Presidio Dr
Tubac, AZ 85646
520-398-9231

Mesquite Valley Growers
8005 East Speedway Boulevard
Tucson, AZ 85710
520-721-8600

Miles' To Go Cactus and Succulent Webalog
520-682-7272, www.miles2go.com

Mountain States Wholesale Nursery
(wholesale only, but website is excellent source of information)
Litchfield Park, AZ
800-840-8509, www.mswn.com

Native Seeds/SEARCH (seeds)
526 North 4th Avenue
Tucson, AZ 85705
520-622-5561, www.nativeseeds.org

Plants for the Southwest
50 East Blacklidge Drive
Tucson, AZ 85705
520-628-8773

Pottery Blow Out
3840 East Grant Road
Tucson, AZ 85716
520-325-6683, www.potteryblowout.com

Shady Way Gardens
566 West Superstition Boulevard
Apache Junction, AZ 85220
480-288-9655

Southwest Gardener
2809 North 15th Avenue
Phoenix, AZ 85007
602-279-9510, www.southwestgardener.com

Starr Nursery
3340 West Ruthann Road
Tucson, AZ 85745
520-743-7052, www.starr-nursery.com

Sticky Situation
Tucson, AZ
520-743-9761, www.stickysituation.com

Tanque Verde Greenhouses
10810 East Tanque Verde Road
Tucson, AZ 85749
520-749-4414, www.cactus-mall.com/tanque-verde/

Tohono Chul Park
7366 North Paseo del Norte
Tucson, AZ 85704
520-742-6455, www.tohonochulpark.org

Tucson Botanical Gardens
2150 North Alvernon Way
Tucson, AZ 85712
520-326-9686, www.tucsonbotanical.org

California

California Cactus Center
216 South Rosemead Boulevard
Pasadena, CA 91107
626-795-2788, www.cactuscenter.com

Grounded
897 South Coast Highway 101, Suite 105
Encinitas, CA 92024,
760-230-1563, www.shopgrounded.com

Lotusland
695 Ashley Rd
Santa Barbara, CA 93108-1059
805-969-9990, www.lotusland.org

Mountain Valley Growers (organic herbs)
38325 Pepperweed Road
Squaw Valley, CA 93675
559-338-2775
www.mountainvalleygrowers.com

San Marcos Growers
125 South San Marcos Road
Santa Barbara, CA 93160
805-683-1561, www.smgrowers.com

Santa Barbara Botanic Garden
1212 Mission Canyon Road
Santa Barbara, CA 93105
805-682-4726, www.sbbg.org

Colorado

Denver Botanic Gardens
1005 York Street
Denver, CO 80206
720-865-3500, www.botanicgardens.org

Nevada

The Springs Preserve (botanical gardens)
333 S. Valley View Boulevard
Las Vegas, NV 89107
702-822-7700, www.springspreserve.org

New Mexico

Bernardo Beach Native Plants
3729 Arno Street Northeast
Albuquerque, NM 87107
505-345-6248,
www.bernardobeachnatives.com

Plants of the Southwest
3095 Agua Fria Road
Santa Fe, NM 87507
505-438-8888,
www.plantsofthesouthwest.com

Santa Fe Greenhouses/High Country Gardens
2902 Rufina Street
Santa Fe, NM 87507
800-925-9387, www.highcountrygardens.com

Texas

Barton Springs Nursery
3601 Bee Caves Road
Austin, TX 78746-5513
512-328-6655
www.bartonspringsnursery.com

Big Red Sun Nursery
1102 East Cesar Chavez Street
Austin, TX 78702
512-480-0688, www.bigredsun.com

Yucca Do Nursery
info@yuccado.com
P.O .Box 1039, Giddings, TX 78942
979-542-8811, www.yuccado.com

Utah

American Specialty Glass (glass mulch)
829 North 400 West
North Salt Lake, UT 84054
877-294-4222,
www.americanspecialtyglass.com

Willard Bay Gardens
7095 South Highway 89
Willard, Utah 84340-9505
435-723-1834 / 801-782-8984,
www.willardbaygardens.com

GENERAL INDEX

Page numbers in boldface denote photographs.

annuals (*also see* wildflowers), 72-80
birds, attracting (*also see* hummingbirds, attracting), 79
butterflies, attracting, 68, 78, 82
cachepots, cachepotting, 21
cantera stone, 18
cast concrete containers, 18, 19
ceramic pots, 17, 19
chiles, roasting, 89
cold temperatures, 11
cool-season color, *see* fall/winter color
cool-season herbs, 83
cool-season veggies, 87, 88
drainage, 28
drip irrigation, 106
edible flowers, 80
fall/winter color, 78
fertilizing, 79, 107-108
 cacti and succulents, 46
 palms and cycads, 53
fiberglass pots, 18, 19
fountains, 24
fragrant plants, 71, 83
goldfinches, attracting, 79
hanging baskets, 19
hanging pots, *see* hanging baskets
heat, 11, 30
hummingbirds, attracting, 67, 79, 82
hypertufa containers, **16,** 19
insulating pots, 30, 31-32
lemony herbs, 84
light conditions, 12
livestock tanks as containers, 86
metal containers, 18, 19
microclimates, 7, 9
moisture, 11
moisture, lack of, 11
moving pots, tips, 24-25
mulch, 105, 111-115
Native Seeds/SEARCH, 90
ollas, 106
plastic pots, 17, 19
porosity of pots, 15, 102
potting soil, 93-99
resin containers, 17
rootstock, citrus, 90
seasonal color, 77-79
shade conditions, 11, 12
size of pot, and watering, 104
size of pot, determining, 27
soil mixes, 87, 93-99
Southwest "sense of place", 7, 45-46
sphagnum moss, 19
spring/summer color, 79
stone containers, 18, 19
strawberry jars, 20
terra-cotta pots, **16**-17, 19
 high-fired vs. low-fired, 16
 quality, 16, 17
 stains, white, 16
trough-style planters, stock tank, **16, 91**
vines, 50, 71, 72
warm-season color, *see* spring/summer color
warm-season herbs, 83
warm-season veggies, 87, 88
watering, 79, 90, 101-106
 agaves, bear grasses, hesperaloes, and yuccas, 47
 aloes, 47
 cacti and succulents, 46
 herbs, 81
watering wands, 105
weird plants, 60-61
wildflowers, 76
wood containers, 18, 19

INDEX OF PLANT NAMES

Abutilon palmeri, 66
Adam's tree, 60
Adenium spp., 39
Agastache, 63
Agastache 'Desert Sunrise', 66, 67, 71
agave, 48, 56
Agave,
 americana var. *mediopicta,* **9**
 attenuata x *ocahui* 'Blue Glow', 56
 bracteosa, 39, 57
 colorata, 56
 deserti, 56
 geminiflora, 39, 57
 macroacantha, 56
 ocahui, 56
 ovatifolia, 57
 parryi, **7,** 57

parryi var. *truncata,* 56
potatorum, 56
schidigera 'Durango Delight', 56
victoriae-reginae, 57
vilmoriniana, 57
Ageratum corymbosum, 64, **68**
Alcea rosea, 78
aloe, 22, 47, 51, 53, 61
Aloe,
barbadensis, 61
dichotoma, 61
ferox, **51,** 61
striata, 61
variegata, 61
x 'Blue Elf', **11, 53,** 61
aloe, medicinal, **22,** 61
alyssum, *see* sweet alyssum
Antirrhinum majus, 79
Aporocactus flagelliformis, 20
Aquilegia chrysantha, 66
Argentine saguaro, **50**
Aristolochia watsonii, 68, 72
Arizona rainbow hedgehog cactus, 38, 58, 76
artichoke agave, 56
Asclepias curassavica, **64,** 68
Asclepias subulata, 65, 68
Asparagus densiflorus 'Myers', 72
Asparagus densiflorus 'Sprengeri', 72
asparagus fern, **36,** 72
Astrophytum myriostigma, 60
Astrophytum ornatum, 61
autumn sage, **64,** 67
Baja fire barrel, 49, 57, 76
Baja "Punk Rock Hairdo" barrel cactus, **48,** 49, 57
banana yucca, 56
barrel cacti, 48, 57-58
baseball plant, **38, 46,** 54
beaked yucca, 56, 71
bear grass, 48, 56
beavertail prickly pear, 59
bell-flowered hesperaloe, 56
Beloperone guttata, 67, 70
Berlandiera lyrata, 64, 71
big pink pincushion, **22**
bishop's cap, **22,** 52, 60
blanket flower, 79
bloodflower, **64,** 68
blue dicks, 62
'Blue Elf' aloe, **11, 53,** 61
'Blue Glow' agave, **37,** 56
blue mist flower, 64, 68
boojum tree, **41,** 60
bougainvillea, dwarf, **10**
Bougainvillea 'Rosenka', 63, 72
Bougainvillea 'Silhouette', 63, 72
Bougainvillea 'Torch Glow', 63, 72
Brahea armata, 62
Brahea edulis, 62
Brassica spp., 78
bulbine, 60
Bulbine frutescens, 60
burro tail, **20**
Bursera microphylla, 60
butterfly agave, 56
cabbage, ornamental, **78**
calendula, 78
Calendula officinalis, 78
Calibanus hookeri, 60
Calibrachoa, **78**
candelilla, 20, 54
cape aloe, 61
Capsicum annuum, 79
Capsicum annuum var. *aviculare,* 90
Catharanthus roseus, 79
Celosia spp., 78
Cephalocereus senilis, 59
Cereus hildmannianus, 58
Cereus hildmannianus f. *tortuosus,* 61
Cereus peruvianus var. *monstrose,* **9**
Chamaerops humilis, 62
chiltepin, 90
chocolate flower, 64, 71
citrus, 89-90
kumquats, 89
limes, 89
lemons, Meyer, 89
orange, trifoliate (rootstock), 89, 90
claret cup, 58
Cleistocactus strausii, 39, 59
climbing janusia, 72
cockscomb, 78
columnar cacti, 50, 58
Cooper's rain lily, 62, 63
coral aloe, 61
coral fountain, 65, 67
coreopsis, 78, 79
Coreopsis tinctoria, 78, 79
cosmos, **73,** 75 nc., 78, 79
Cosmos (spp.), 78
Cosmos bipinnatus, 79
Cosmos sulphureus, 79

creosote bush, 51
crown of thorns, 55
cycads, 53, 62
Cycas revoluta, 62
Delosperma cooperi, **100**
desert agave 56
desert bluebells, 76
desert milkweed, 65, 68
Dianthus barbatus, 79, 80
Dichelostemma pulchellum, 62
Dichondra argentea, 47
Dicliptera suberecta, 67, 71
Dioon edule, 39, 62
Dioon spinulosum, 62
Dioons, **53**
dogweed, 65, 68
donkey tail, 20
'Durango Delight' agave, 56
dwarf palmetto, 62
Echeveria spp., 20
Echinocactus grusonii, 58, 76
Echinocereus
  engelmannii, 58
  fendleri, **49**
  nicholii, 58, 76
  rigidissimus, 38, 58, 76
  triglochidiatus 'White Sands Strain', 58
Echinopsis terscheckii, **50**
elephant tree, 60
elephant's food, 20, **30 n.,** 60
Engelmann's prickly pear, 51, 59
'Epic' torch cactus, 49
Eremophila maculata Valentine®, 67, 71
Erythrina flabelliformis, 51, 61
Eschscholzia mexicana, **9,** 76
Euphorbia, 54
  antisyphilitica, 20, 54
  esulenta, 55
  ingens, 54
  milii, 55
  obesa, 38, 54
  pulcherima, 54
  resinifera, 55
  rigida, 66
Eustoma grandiflorum, 79
Fendler's hedgehog, **49**
ferns, 72
Ferocactus,
  gracilis var. *coloratus,* 57, 76
  pringlei, 57, 76
  rectispinus, 58
  stainsii, 57
  wislizeni, 58
Ficus petiolaris, 61
fire barrel, 48, 57, 76, **112**
firewheel, 65, 79
fishhook barrel, 58
Fouquieria, 52
  columnaris, 60
  diguetii, 60
  macdougalii, 60
  splendens, 51, 60
foxtail fern, 72, **110**
Gaillardia aristata, 65
Gaillardia pulchella, 79
Gaillardia spp., **66**
Gaura lindheimeri 'Pink Cloud', 71
geranium (*also see* scented geraniums), 75
giant candelabra tree, 54
giant hesperaloe, 51, 56
Glandularia pulchella, 68
globe amaranth, 79
golden barrel, **23, 40,** 48, 58, 76
golden columbine, **65,** 66
golden hedgehog, 58, 76
golden sage 'Aurea', **80**
Gomphrena globosa, 79
gopher plant, 66
gorilla's armpit, **52,** 60
gourds, 88
grizzly bear prickly pear, 59, **103**
Guadalupe palm, 62
hedgehog cacti, 38, 49, 58
hens and chicks, 20
herbs, **6,** 80-85
  Allium spp., 83
  Anethum graveolens, 82, 83
  Apiaceae, 82
  basil, 82, **83,** 85
  borage, 82, 84
  caraway, 82, 84
  caraway thyme, 84
  catnip, 83
  Chamaemelum nobile, 83
  chamomile, annual German, 83, 84
  chamomile, perennial Roman, 83
  chervil, 82
  chives, 83
  cilantro, 82, 83, 84, 85
  conehead thyme, 84
  Coriandrum sativum, 83, 85
  creeping thyme, 84

dill, 82, 83, 84
Dysphania ambrosioides, 83, 85
English thyme, 84
epazote, 83, 85
fennel, 82
Foeniculum vulgare, 82
garlic chives, 83
Lavandula multifida, 67
Lavandula spp., 67, 71, 83, 84
lavender, 67, 71, 81, 83, 84
lavender, fernleaf, 67
lemon balm, 83, 84
lemon basil, 84
lemon bergamot mint, 85
lemon grass, 85
lemon thyme, 84, 85
lemon verbena, 85
Matricaria recutita, 83
Melissa officinalis, 83
Mentha spp., 83, 84
Mexican oregano, 67, 68, **69,** 71
mint, 83, 84
Nepeta cataria, 83
Ocimum spp., 83, 85
oregano, 83, 84
Origanum spp., 83, 84
parsley, 82, 84
Petroselinum crispum, 84
Petroselinum graveolens, 82, 84
Poliomintha maderensis, 67
rosemary, 82, 83, 84
Rosmarinus officinalis, 83, 84
sage, 84
thyme, 81, 83, 84
Thymus capitata, 84
Thymus herba-barona, 84
Thymus praecox subsp. *arcticus,* 84
Thymus spp., 83, 84
Thymus vulgaris, 84
Thymus x *citriodorus,* 84
hesperaloe, 48, 56
Hesperaloe campanulata, 56
Hesperaloe funifera, 51, 56
Hesperaloe parviflora, 51, 57
hollyhock, 38, 78
hummingbird mint, 63, 66, 67, 71
hummingbird mint, hybrid, 66
Iceland poppy, 78
Indian mallow, 66, **67**
Ipomoea coccinea, 67, 72
Janusia gracilis, 72
Jerusalem sage, 67
jet-tipped agave, 56
Johnny-jump-up, 78, 80
Justicia brandegeana, **70**
kale, ornamental, **38**, 78
kokerbom, 61
Lantana montevidensis, 68, **70**
lantana, purple, **70**
lantana, yellow, **75**
Lathyrus odoratus, 79
lavender, *see under* herbs
lemon-scented geranium, 85
lemon verbena, 85
lisianthus, 79
lobelia, 75, 78
Lobelia erinus, 78
Lobularia maritima, 79
Lophocereus schottii, 59
'Macho Mocha' mangave, **37,** 60
Madagascar periwinkle, 79
Mammillaria guelzowiana, **22**
Mammillaria parkinsonii, 60
Manfreda maculosa, 61
Manfreda x 'Macho Mocha', 60
marigold, 72, 79
Mathiola incana, 79
Maurandya antirrhiniflora, 72
mealy cup sage, 68, 75
medicinal aloe, 61
Mediterranean fan palm, 62
Medusa's head, 55
mescal ceniza, 56
Mexican blue palm, 62
Mexican evening primrose, 68
Mexican fencepost, 47, 58
Mexican gold poppy, **9,** 76, **102**
Mexican hairy barrel, 48-49, 58
Mexican sunflower, 78, 79
Mexican tree ocotillo, **41,** 52, 60
milk-chocolate spine prickly pear, 39, 59
milkweed vine, 68, 72
million bells, **78**
Morea polystacha, 63
Mormon tea, 51
Moroccan mound, 55
moss rose, *see* rose moss
moss verbena, 68
nasturtium, 38, 78, 80
nerine, 62
Nerine filamentosa, 62
nicotiana, 78

Nicotiana alata, 78
Nierembergia gracilis 'Starry Eyes', 70
night-blooming cereus, 58
Nolina microcarpa, 56
Notocactus leninghausii, **38**
ocahui, 56
ocotillo, 50, **51, 52,** 60, 71
octopus agave, 57
Oenothera speciosus, 68
Old Man of Mexico, 59
Old Man of the Andes, 39, 58
Old Man of the Mountain, 59
Opuntia
basilaris, 59
engelmannii, 51, 59
erinacea, 59
violacea gosseliniana, 39, 59
violacea macrocentra, 39, 59
violacea santa-rita, 59
Oreocereus celsianus, 39, 58
Oreocereus trollii, 59
organ pipe cactus, 50, 59
owl's eyes, 60
oxblood lily, 63
Pachycereus marginatus, 58
Pachycereus schottii var. *monstrous,* 59
Pachypodium spp., 39
pale-leaf yucca, 57
palma de la virgen, 39, 62
palms, 53, 62
pansy, 75, 78
Pansy x *wittrockiana,* 78
Papaver nudicaule, 78
Papaver rhoeas, 79
Parry's agave, **7, 17,** 57
partridge breast aloe, 61
peacock iris, 63
Pedilanthus macrocarpus, 51, 61
Pelargonium spp., 83, 84
pentas, 78
Pentas lanceolata, 78
peppers, ornamental, 79
petunia, 75, 78
Petunia hybrids, 78
Phacelia campanularia, 76
Phlomis fruticosa, 67
phlox, 79
Phlox drummondii, 79
Phoenix robelenii, 62
pink rain lily, **63**
poinsettia, 54
Poliomintha maderensis, 67, **69,** 71
Poncirus trifoliate, 90
Portulaca x hybrids, 79
Portulacaria afra, 20, **30,** 60
'Prairie Sunset' rain lily, 63
prickly pears, **50**, 51, 59
pygmy date palm, 62
Queen Victoria agave, 57, **102**
queen's wreath, 50
rain lilies, 47, **63**
rat-tail cactus, 20
red devil verbena, 70
red hesperaloe, 51, 57
Rhodophiala bifida, 63
rock fig, 61
rose moss, **73, 75,** 79
'Rosenka' bougainvillea, 72
Russelia equisetiformis, 65, 67
Sabal minor, 62
Sabal uresana, 62
sages, 83, 84
sago palm, 62
Salvia,
coccinea, 79
farinacea, 68
farinacea 'Victoria Blue', 79
greggii, **64,** 67
'Ultra Violet', 71
Salvia spp., 83
Santa Rita prickly pear, 59
Sarcostemma cynanchoides, 68, 72
scarlet creeper, 67, 72
scented geraniums, 82, 83, 84, 85
Scutellaria 'Violet Cloud', 71
Sedum morganianum, 20
senita, 59
Shirley poppy, 79
shrimp plant, 67, **70**
'Silhouette' bougainvillea, 72
silver pony-foot, 47
slipper plant, **39,** 51, 61
snapdragon, 75, 79
snapdragon vine, **71,** 72
snow pole, 39, 59
Sonoran palmetto, 62
southwest coral bean, 51, 61
southwestern pipevine, 68, 72
spider agave, 39, **48,** 57
spiny dioon, 62
spurges, 54
Stachys coccinea, 67, 70

star cactus, 61
'Starry Eyes' nierembergia, 70
Stenocereus thurberi, 59
stock, 75, 79
strawberry hedgehog, 58
succulent bulbs, 62
sweet alyssum, 75, 79
sweet pea, 79
sweet William, 79, 80
Tagetes erecta, 79
Tagetes patula, 79
Texas betony, 67, 70
Texas tuberose, 61
Thymophylla pentachaeta, 65, 68
Tithonia rotundifolia, 78, 79
torch cacti, 58
torch cactus hybrids, 49, 58
'Torch Glow' bougainvillea, 72
totempole cactus, 59
trailing lantana, 68, 70
Trichocereus hybrids, 58
Tropaeolum majus, 78, 80
tropical sage, 79
tuxedo spine prickly pear, 39, 59
twin-flowered agave, 39, 57
twisted cereus, 61
twisted yucca, 57
'Ultra Violet' sage, 71
'Valentine' emu bush, 67, 71
veggies, 86-89
  amaranth, 88
  arugula, 88
  Asian broccoli, 88
  Asian greens, 88
  beans, 88
  beets, 88
  bok choi, 88
  broccoli, 88
  broccoli raab, 88
  Brussels sprouts, 88
  cabbage, 88
  carrot, 88
  cauliflower, 88
  chiles, 88, **89**
  Chinese cabbage, 88
  collard greens, 88
  corn, 88
  cucumber, 88
  eggplant, 88
  garlic, 88
  kale, 88
  kohlrabi, 88
  leek, 88
  lettuce, 87, 88
  melons, 88
  mustard greens, 88
  okra, 88
  onion, 88
  peas, 88
  peppers, 88
  radish, 87, 88
  spinach, 88
  summer squash, 88
  Swiss chard, 88
  tomatoes, **88**
  turnips, 88
velvet honeysuckle, 67, 71
Verbena peruviana 'Red', 70
verbena, red devil, 70
'Victoria Blue' sage, 79
vinca, **75,** 79
vines, 50, 71, 72
viola, 79
Viola cornuta, 79
Viola tricolor, 78, 80
'Violet Cloud' skullcap, 71
'Volcano Sunrise' torch cactus, 49
whale's tongue agave, 57
whirling butterflies, 71
white stripe agave, **9**
yucca, **9**, 48, 50, 56
Yucca,
  baccata, 56,
  pallida, 57
  rostrata, 56
  rupicola, 57
Zephyranthes drummondii, 62, 63
Zephyranthes grandiflora, 63
Zephyranthes spp., 47, 63
Zephyranthes x 'Prairie Sunset', 63
zinnia, **73,** 78, 79
Zinnia angustifolia, 79
Zinnia elegans, 79
Zinnia, spp., 78

Rio Nuevo Publishers®
P.O. Box 5250, Tucson, Arizona 85703-0250
(520) 623-9558, www.rionuevo.com

Library of Congress Cataloging-in-Publication Data

Calhoun, Scott.
Hot pots : container gardening in the arid Southwest / Scott Calhoun and Lynn Hassler.
p. cm.
Includes index.
ISBN-13: 978-1-933855-39-4 (pbk. : alk. paper)
ISBN-10: 1-933855-39-8 (pbk. : alk. paper) 1. Container gardening—Southwestern States. 2. Container gardening—Southwestern States—Equipment and supplies. I. Hassler, Lynn. II. Title.
SB418.C35 2009
635.9'860979—dc22

2009028657

Design: Karen Schober, Seattle, Washington

Printed in Korea.

10 9 8 7 6 5 4 3 2 1